Meeting Community Needs

PRACTICAL GUIDES FOR LIBRARIANS

About the Series

This innovative series written and edited for librarians by librarians provides authoritative, practical information and guidance on a wide spectrum of library processes and operations.

Books in the series are focused, describing practical and innovative solutions to a problem facing today's librarian and delivering step-by-step guidance for planning, creating, implementing, managing, and evaluating a wide range of services and programs.

The books are aimed at beginning and intermediate librarians needing basic instruction/guidance in a specific subject and at experienced librarians who need to gain knowledge in a new area or guidance in implementing a new program/service.

About the Series Editor

The **Practical Guides for Librarians** series was conceived by and is edited by M. Sandra Wood, MLS, MBA, AHIP, FMLA, librarian emerita, Penn State University Libraries.

M. Sandra Wood was a librarian at the George T. Harrell Library, the Milton S. Hershey Medical Center, College of Medicine, Pennsylvania State University, Hershey, PA, for more than thirty-five years, specializing in reference, educational, and database services. Ms. Wood worked for several years as a development editor for Neal-Schuman Publishers.

Ms. Wood received an MLS from Indiana University and an MBA from the University of Maryland. She is a fellow of the Medical Library Association and served as a member of MLA's Board of Directors from 1991 to 1995. Ms. Wood is founding and current editor of *Medical Reference Services Quarterly*, now in its thirty-fifth volume. She also was founding editor of the *Journal of Consumer Health on the Internet* and the *Journal of Electronic Resources in Medical Libraries* and served as editor/coeditor of both journals through 2011.

Titles in the Series

1. *How to Teach: A Practical Guide for Librarians* by Beverley E. Crane.

2. *Implementing an Inclusive Staffing Model for Today's Reference Services* by Julia K. Nims, Paula Storm, and Robert Stevens.

3. *Managing Digital Audiovisual Resources: A Practical Guide for Librarians* by Matthew C. Mariner.

Meeting Community Needs

A Practical Guide for Librarians

Pamela H. MacKellar

PRACTICAL GUIDES FOR LIBRARIANS, NO. 21

ROWMAN & LITTLEFIELD
Lanham • Boulder • New York • London

Published by Rowman & Littlefield
A wholly owned subsidiary of The Rowman & Littlefield Publishing Group, Inc.
4501 Forbes Boulevard, Suite 200, Lanham, Maryland 20706
www.rowman.com

Unit A, Whitacre Mews, 26-34 Stannary Street, London SE11 4AB

British Library Cataloguing in Publication Information Available

Library of Congress Cataloging-in-Publication Data
Name: MacKellar, Pamela H., author.
Title: Meeting community needs : a practical guide for librarians / Pamela H. MacKellar.
Description: Lanham : Rowman & Littlefield, [2016] | Series: Practical guides for librarians ; no. 21 | Includes bibliographical references and index.
Identifiers: LCCN 2015031375| ISBN 9780810893276 (hardcover : alk. paper) | ISBN 9780810891340 (pbk. : alk. paper) | ISBN 9780810891357 (ebook)
Subjects: LCSH: Libraries and community. | Libraries—Aims and objectives. | Library planning. | Public services (Libraries)—Evaluation.
Classification: LCC Z716.4 .M32 2015 | DDC 021.2—dc23 LC record available at http://lccn.loc.gov/2015031375

∞™ The paper used in this publication meets the minimum requirements of American National Standard for Information Sciences—Permanence of Paper for Printed Library Materials, ANSI/NISO Z39.48-1992.

Printed in the United States of America

This book is dedicated to librarians who want to make a difference for *all* of the people they serve—in their communities, schools, colleges and universities, corporations, prisons, hospitals, law offices, or wherever their libraries may be.

Contents

List of Illustrations

⊚ Figures

Tables

Preface

Today's libraries are customer-centered portals of knowledge and learning for entire communities, and a librarian's work is to make a difference in people's lives by meeting community needs. Because library programs and services are no longer confined to physical library buildings, the potential for meeting the needs of more people has been unleashed. Librarianship involves interacting with entire communities and constantly engaging in meaningful ways with the people in them. Meeting various changing needs in myriad ways keeps a librarian's job interesting, challenging, and even exciting. The rewards are visible and measurable. Communities are reaping huge benefits. Librarians are being recognized and included as valuable and respected partners, collaborators, and astute problem solvers in our towns, schools, universities, and corporations. It is about time!

Long ago, libraries were essentially book warehouses. Librarians were in charge of organizing and managing inventories and monitoring the people who entered the library to use the inventory. Some supplemented traditional library services by providing educational programs to promote knowledge and learning. They were uber-focused on what was going on inside the library, and they took their jobs seriously. To demonstrate their worth, they generated endless statistics about how many books they cataloged and circulated, the number of people entering the building, the number of reference questions asked, or how many people attended programs. Librarians could use this method for measuring effectiveness as long as their jobs revolved around organizing and managing inventories and monitoring people inside the library; however, at some point libraries evolved into community knowledge centers accessible from anywhere. Then the focus of their work shifted from minding the inner workings of the library to meeting the needs of people in the community at large.

Savvy librarians are now meeting community needs and determining effectiveness by measuring the degree to which their programs and services are making the intended difference for people. Unfortunately, too many librarians are still counting things and providing programs they have offered for decades because "it has always worked in the past." Some state library agencies are still training librarians to evaluate and measure what is happening in the library as a way to assess community needs. This is unacceptable. It makes no sense. We are in the present. Librarians stuck in the past working from an outdated model are doing their communities and their profession a disservice.

Meeting Community Needs: A Practical Guide for Librarians is designed for librarians in all library types. Being effective requires being in close touch with your community whether it is a city, town, or village; college or university; public or private school; or corporation, hospital, or business. It requires understanding what information the people you serve need, how they access information, how they use it, how it benefits them, and how they share it. Effectiveness is delivering the services and programs that people need in ways they can use them to improve their lives. Although communities differ in their makeup, the same principles apply whether your library serves residents in a town, students in a university, teachers in a school, or employees in a corporation. Effective programs and services make a measurable difference for people by meeting their needs—whoever they are and whatever their needs.

Providing library programs and services for your entire population is more important than ever. Librarians working in libraries of all types must provide programs and services that meet community needs if libraries are to stay relevant and survive in the long run. Librarians cannot rely on the idea that "everyone loves libraries" so they will always have enough money to operate. This is a false notion that is not sustainable. If you are concerned mainly about keeping the library in operation, adequately funded, and fully staffed without relating these "library needs" to how the community will benefit, you are missing the point. When you provide effective programs and services, and measure their effectiveness, you can use hard facts to prove the difference the library is making in the community. Librarians must be able to measure their success and demonstrate the library's worth with verifiable proof if they are going to be competitive for available funds in the future.

Meeting Community Needs presents a process that will require a paradigm shift for those who are accustomed to concentrating on what is going on inside the library above meeting real community needs. If you think that skyrocketing statistics prove your library is thriving, brace yourself. This book will make you take a serious look at how well library programs and services are meeting your community's needs. Library work is primarily about making a difference for people. It is time to connect with your community and take action. The process explained here will show you the way.

Objectives and Organization

The purpose of *Meeting Community Needs* is to help librarians adapt to an evolved library model by showing them how to approach effectiveness in terms of providing programs and services that make a difference. It offers a community-centered, practical approach that will help you improve the lives of people in your community and demonstrate the library's value when it counts. It dispels outdated notions and rationales left over from the past by offering a logical step-by-step process with clear explanations and examples. At the end you will wonder why it took you so long to embrace this approach. Librarians who use *Meeting Community Needs* will:

- Understand the meaning of effectiveness and how to measure it
- Know how to determine what their communities need
- Understand how to design programs and services intended to meet needs
- Understand how what they do contributes to meeting community needs

- Have the information they need to produce positive outcomes for people
- Gain a renewed belief in the value of libraries
- Have the confidence they need to promote the value of the library
- Be able to compete for funding on equal terms
- Understand how committing to the process can help them do their jobs more effectively

The information inside is divided into three parts. Part I, "Discovering What Your Community Needs," focuses on the idea that the roles of libraries must change as they respond to changing community needs. It illustrates how to get started by looking at your library's role and mission, your community, and what people need. This knowledge prepares you to plan effective programs and services.

- Chapter 1, "Library Services and Programming in the Twenty-First Century," covers the evolution of libraries, the influence of technology on libraries, and the meaning of effective programs and services today. Librarians who are focused on fulfilling the library's mission and meeting people's needs are equipped to provide effective programs and services. They use technology as a tool to help them meet community needs. This chapter stresses the importance of responding rapidly to changing community needs if libraries are to remain relevant.
- Chapter 2, "Clarifying the Library's Role," introduces a process for discovering library programs and services that meet community needs. The first step is to clarify the library's role, purpose, or mission. Without a meaningful mission, librarians cannot provide effective programs and services. Mission statements guide the way when community needs change and new technology emerges. This chapter includes examples of mission statements from libraries and other entities, and an exercise to help readers review, revise, or compose their own library's mission statement.
- Chapter 3, "Creating a Community Profile," covers the second step in the process for discovering library programs and services. Community profiles help you to understand the overall nature of your community and what the people there need. This chapter includes a valuable Community Profile Worksheet with questions to answer about your community, as well as resources for finding existing community data, and a community profile example.
- Chapter 4, "Assessing Community Needs," guides you through a process for discovering community needs that are within the parameters of the library's mission. Community needs assessments are necessary prior to planning relevant library programs and services. This chapter clarifies the meanings of some commonly misunderstood terms— "community needs," "user needs," and "library needs"—and stresses the fact that communities include library nonusers as well as users. This understanding is essential prior to conducting a useful assessment. The chapter includes some preliminary questions to ask before you conduct an assessment and explains various assessment methodologies. Look for links to useful needs assessment examples.
- Chapter 5, "Organizing, Analyzing, and Interpreting Assessment Results," leads you through ways to deal with the data you collected in the assessment. The methods vary depending on the instruments you used for the assessment; however, the objective is to turn the raw data into useful information for determining what programs and services to offer. The chapter covers assessment reports, which summarize results

and make conclusions that are useful in the planning process; prioritizing needs; and making decisions about which needs the library will address in the coming years. It includes examples to illustrate descriptive statistics, identifying categories, and prioritizing needs.

Part II, "Planning Services and Programs That Make a Difference," addresses how to use the information about your community that you compiled, gathered, and analyzed in part I to design effective programs and services.

- Chapter 6, "Designing Effective Programs and Services," delves into the exciting and creative planning phase. This is where you design innovative ways to meet the needs of your specific community. No more one size fits all programming! Your hard work will pay off as you see how the library's mission, the community needs you decide to meet, and the programs and services you offer are all interconnected. You will learn about the seven basic core elements every successful program and service needs.
- Chapter 7, "Developing Goals, Objectives, and Outcomes," guides you through the first steps of program design. It covers how to establish goals that are meant to meet needs and generate program ideas with others. Defining SMART (Specific, Measurable, Achievable, Realistic, and Time-Bound) objectives allows the program or service to take shape and creates a way to measure your results. This chapter stresses the importance of identifying outcomes, or how people will benefit. It is important to include partners and collaborators who can share the responsibilities of funding, expertise, and resources.
- Chapter 8, "Determining Activities, Staff Requirements, and Time Line," leads readers through the next steps in the program design process. This is the heart of program and service design. You will learn how to determine how a program or service will function by listing every activity required to complete a program or implement a service, determining who will do the work, and estimating how long it will take them. It is essential to investigate other programs like yours to avoid common pitfalls. This chapter provides the information you need to create a time line for your project or service that will help you understand the sequence of activities and track your progress.
- Chapter 9, "Creating a Program Budget," covers one of the most important aspects of planning services and programs. Budgets help you determine all the resources that are necessary for success. You will learn how to create and combine a personnel budget and a non-personnel budget using examples as guides. The chapter covers the usefulness of program budgets versus line-item budgets for libraries that are focused on meeting community needs. Once you know the resources you need, you can find them.
- Chapter 10, "Funding Effective Programs and Services," provides different approaches for funding library services and programs. It is important to know your options to avoid being blocked at this point because "the library doesn't have the money." Options include finding money in the library's budget, forming partnerships, working with friends' groups or library foundations, and seeking grants. This chapter outlines grant sources and resources, and the basics of researching grants. It suggests a new funding model in which librarians first focus on community needs, then actively seek the funding required to meet the needs.

Part III, "Providing Effective Programs and Services and Measuring Your Success," concerns the work involved in offering programs and services, and how to use your experience to move into the future.

- Chapter 11, "Implementing Library Programs and Services," is doing the work that makes the program happen. This is when all your preparation and planning come to fruition. Preliminary implementation activities include naming the program, making a workspace, hiring staff, purchasing supplies and equipment, and updating the time line. This chapter covers the essentials of effective program management and basic project management principles that librarians can use.
- Chapter 12, "Measuring Effectiveness," provides an overview of the basic evaluation methodologies for librarians to use for measuring the effectiveness of programs and services. Evaluation is necessary to determine the degree to which you have achieved your objectives. It tells you what to do next. This chapter covers how to choose the right evaluation method, organizing and analyzing data, and communicating results. Evaluation tells you how to adjust or modify a program or service for better success, or when to discontinue a program. When you are informed by evaluation you can allocate library resources accordingly.
- Chapter 13, "Using Your Success to Move Forward," stresses that meeting community needs by providing effective programs and services is an ongoing process. You will experience natural benefits—the most important is meeting community needs and making a difference for people. Secondarily, you will have a renewed passion for your work, you will be more involved with the community, and you will know why you are doing what you are doing. Librarians who use this process will have in place many elements that are required for grant funding. Marketing the library will come naturally as you share your successes inside and outside the library. This chapter introduces an established continuous improvement model that librarians can use to incorporate this process into their work.

Meeting Community Needs: A Practical Guide for Librarians includes illustrations, worksheets, and checklists throughout to enhance the learning experience.

How To Use This Book

The steps in this book must be completed in order. The logic to the sequence of the steps will become apparent as you do the work. For instance, the first steps involve creating a community profile and assessing community needs. This is because you must know about your community and what people need in order to design programs and services to meet the needs. Do not skip around in this book or you will be confused.

Because every library serves a different population with unique needs, no single formula or set of services and programs will be effective for every library. You can't follow a template from another library. Programs and services that are right for one population may be wrong for another. Worksheets and examples in this book and on the Internet will give you ideas about where to start. Do not copy them without doing the work or you will defeat the purpose.

Providing effective programs and services requires doing the work, beginning with assessing your community's needs. This book serves as a roadmap to help you understand

and implement a process of providing effective library programs and services that are responsive to your community's specific needs. Along the way you will need to make many decisions that are unique to your community and library. Some decisions will be challenging. You must do this work yourself, often with help from the board, community members, business leaders, and other stakeholders.

Whether you are undertaking this endeavor alone, with a small planning committee, or a large organizational group with many subcommittees, the concepts are the same. Select the parts that apply to you and use them to move the library forward. Break the process into manageable segments that are realistic for you to complete. If you are a solo librarian, it is probably not feasible to do this work alone in one short time period. It may take a long time and help from others. Be persistent and stick with it. The important thing is to understand why this approach is important and commit to it. Your community will be glad you did.

Acknowledgments

I would like to thank Charles Harmon, acquisitions editor at Rowman & Littlefield, and Sandy Wood, series editor, who continued to believe in me and encourage me, even in the tough times. Sandy, you have the patience of a saint. Thank you also to my husband, Bruce, who always has to dig deep when I am involved in large projects. You are one of a kind.

Part I

DISCOVERING WHAT YOUR COMMUNITY NEEDS

CHAPTER 1

Library Services and Programming in the Twenty-First Century

TODAY, LIBRARIANS WHO PROVIDE EFFECTIVE LIBRARY SERVICES and programs that meet the current needs of the people they serve must rapidly adapt and evolve to stay abreast of their changing communities. Public, academic, school, and special librarians must all be aware of what people need in a library. Demographics are shifting. Technology is affecting the way people access information. The economy has caused new needs to emerge as unemployment rates rise. Corporations have redirected their focus to stay in business. Information needs are changing in communities where:

- People are using mobile technologies to find information
- Employment opportunities and applications are online
- Immigrants have relocated from other countries
- College students are seeking learning communities and electronic information
- All elementary school students do not have Internet access at home
- Scientists share their research via online groups
- School curricula are becoming more standardized

Librarians who make it their business to understand clearly the characteristics of the populations they serve, who are aware of information trends, and who stay current with emerging needs and technologies are equipped to deliver effective library programs and services to meet specific needs.

What librarians do has evolved significantly over time primarily because the needs of people being served by all library types have changed—and continue to change—significantly. Providing relevant programs and services became more challenging for librarians when computers arrived on the scene beginning in the 1970s. Soon librarians were responsible for informing themselves about new technologies and deciding which ones were most appropriate to help them in their work. With the arrival of the Internet in the 1990s came a revolutionary new way for people to communicate and access information. With vastly changing communities and a constant stream of new information technologies to consider, it is fundamentally the library's role or mission that guides the way for librarians.

Defining Library Services and Programming

Library programs and services are central to the library's mission, and they are the forms taken by the library staff to accomplish their work. What a particular library offers is derived from that library's mission and strategic plan. The planning process takes into consideration the needs of the people being served by the library and it identifies the library's goals over a period of time. Planning also involves defining objectives and activities that are designed to accomplish the library's goals. Because strategic plans are meant to guide library staff in meeting the current needs of the community, librarians, the library board, community members, and stakeholders must update the library's plans as the population and their needs change. As plans are updated, library services and programs are adjusted to accommodate people's changing needs.

Library Programs

Library programs are a specific set of group activities sponsored by a library. Programs may be ongoing, a series, or one-time events. Programming expands on a library's physical and digital collections and helps to fulfill a library's mission. Library programs are not one size fits all. Every library offers a unique set of programs because every library serves a unique population with specific needs, every library has a unique plan with specific goals, and every library has its own mission.

Different types of libraries provide different kinds of programs. Public library programs are presented for groups in the community such as children, teens, and adults, and special populations such as seniors, immigrants, and people with disabilities. Regardless of the specific target group, public library programs usually meet the informational, educational, and/or recreational needs of the people being served. Some common public library programs include story hours, book discussion groups, creative writing programs, author readings, lecture series, musical performances, dance performances, movies, dramatic performances, summer reading programs, arts and crafts programs, poetry readings, genealogy workshops, computer training classes, technology instruction, ESL (English as a second language) classes, and employment skills workshops.

Academic library programs usually help support the research and academic needs of students, faculty, and staff. Programs may include library instruction, classes on research practices, information literacy sessions, library orientation programs, digital library programs, and library liaison programs. School library programs support the curriculum by providing programs such as information skills instruction, author visits, and book fairs. Special library programs are provided to meet the informational needs of employees and others served by a library in a corporation, museum, hospital, or research institute, for example. Special libraries may offer instruction on accessing specialized electronic materials and searching subject databases, or they might collaborate with other departments in an organization to hold seminars and author talks, or offer spaces for working collaboratively.

The reason for library programs is to meet people's information needs. Library programming is *not* primarily a way to:

- Market the library
- Get people into the library
- Introduce poor people to cultural events
- Establish goodwill in the community or within your organization
- Increase the library's visibility
- Hold social events
- Raise money for the library

Library Services

Like library programs, library services vary depending on the kind of library. Typically, basic library services in all kinds of libraries include reference, circulation, interlibrary loan, reserves, readers' advisory, computers and technology, copying and printing, digital and electronic services, outreach services, and facilities. Of course, services are designed to meet the current needs of the population being served and to help librarians fulfill the mission or purpose of a particular library.

The fundamental reason for library services and programs is to meet people's information needs.

Understanding How the Internet Has Affected Services and Programs

During the period when computers were introduced in the 1970s, as new technologies emerged in the 1980s, and the Internet arrived on the scene in the early 1990s, it was essential for librarians to be clear about the role of their libraries and the purpose of their work. Librarians who knew what they were doing and why they were doing it prior to the arrival of computers had an easier time when it came to deciding how to incorporate them in the library. As time passed, they became confident about determining which new technologies to implement and effectively using the Internet in their work. In the end, computers, technology, and the Internet are simply alternative ways to communicate or record the written word. They are tools that librarians can use to help them do the work of the library. In the beginning it was essential for librarians to welcome computers, new technology, and the Internet into libraries because they all had an enormous influence on how information was recorded, managed, and accessed. Librarians and library workers who resisted change and refused to embrace the role of computers and new technologies on the entire information field, and on libraries in particular, sealed their own fates, ensuring that their libraries lagged behind from the start.

During the last thirty years of the twentieth century, libraries were changed forever. All aspects of library services were impacted, from internal operations such as collection development, acquisitions, cataloging, and circulation to user services such as access, reference, and outreach. New formats and methods for recording, organizing, accessing, retrieving, synthesizing, and disseminating information exist to help librarians meet people's needs. Librarians retooled their jobs. Automated library systems changed the workflow and redefined job duties. Card catalogs disappeared, and online catalogs took their place. Electronic databases proliferated, and paper journal subscriptions were discontinued. Librarians had to change and adapt or be left behind in the information field.

With all the opportunities new technologies brought for enhancing library services and programs, incorporating them into library operations was admittedly an enormous challenge. It is not so surprising that some librarians may have been overwhelmed—and even confused—by the changes that faced them and the many choices technology made available to them. Furthermore, librarians were tasked with staying up-to-date with new technology and evaluating and selecting the right products to help them in their work. The shift in the library profession was monumental. Some librarians resisted change or lost focus, and others may have temporarily lost track of people's current needs and the library's mission. Others who knew their library's role and who were committed to meeting the needs of the people they served were positioned to navigate this change, assume new and different responsibilities, and use the new innovations to improve library services and programs. These librarians understood that it was not the computers and technology that drove their decisions, but rather the library's purpose and people's needs.

Today, libraries must minimally offer computers and Internet access. The physical library looks much different than it did before computers, with fewer shelves and more computer workstations, fewer books and more learning commons areas. Librarians are responsible for teaching users how to operate computers, search for information on the Internet, use electronic databases, and evaluate electronic information—as well as clearing paper jams, troubleshooting public computer problems, and updating antivirus software in some libraries. Library users want to search the catalog, reserve materials, ask reference questions, download e-books, and renew them online without having to visit the physical library building.

Many library programs employ technology to meet people's needs. For instance, in these difficult economic times, librarians may offer workshops on finding a job on the Internet, how to prepare a résumé using Microsoft Word or complete an online application, and how to establish an e-mail account for communicating with potential employers. According to Wisner (2009), the advent of technology created "the postmodern library—the library plus technology" where children stare at monitors showing videos or stand in lines waiting their turn to play computer games. There is less quiet space, fewer people are browsing the stacks, and reference desks are disappearing. Doll (2013) notes that some libraries have offered programs such as hog-butchering demonstrations, Zumba classes, virtual Wii bowling, and holiday shopping seminars in an attempt to stay relevant in the technological age.

Today, libraries need a web presence to meet the information needs of remote users who want to search catalogs, renew books, download audiobooks and e-books, and access databases from outside the library. "Ask a librarian" online chats have replaced the reference desk, and e-resources are part of every collection. With the abundance of databases that people can access from library websites, librarians are teaching classes or producing online tutorials on how to perform effective database searches. Libraries are offering programs on how to select and use various e-book devices; some have produced video tutorials about how to download e-books from the library's collection.

Knowing What Services and Programs To Offer

Every library has a unique mission, and every community has specific needs. No single formula or set of services and programs works for every library. Programs and services that are right for one population may be wrong for another. A flourishing and valued, vibrant and relevant library is one where librarians and others who do the work of the library are attuned to the community and its needs, and they have a passion for fulfilling the library's unique mission by providing relevant programs and services for the betterment of the community. It is one where librarians stay informed about new technological developments as well as shifts in their communities, and where they continually adjust and change programs and services to meet needs and incorporate innovations.

During times of significant societal shifts that have impacted libraries, information science, and publishing—such as the production of paper; the invention of the printing press; or the advent of computers, information technology, and the Internet—libraries' roles have shifted. When the needs of society were for a place to store written records, libraries stored written records. When people needed to learn new job skills, libraries provided services to support adult education. When students and teachers in public schools needed support in the way of books and other learning materials, school libraries were established to fulfill that role. Today, as computers and new technologies have become an important way to access information, librarians are providing new programs to teach computer skills and how to use the Internet, and implementing services that employ new technologies. As needs evolve or circumstances change, librarians adjust.

In addition to understanding their library's role, librarians are also responsible for staying informed about changing needs in their communities—whether their communities consist of residents in a city, town, or other geographical area; students, faculty, and staff in a college or university; professionals and employees in a hospital, law office, or corporation; prisoners in a prison; or teachers and students in an elementary school. This applies to librarians of all kinds who work in libraries of every type. Common sense, experience, and history tell us that people's information needs change constantly. It follows, then, that in order to provide relevant library services and programs, librarians must be vigilant about keeping abreast of changing needs in their communities.

Along with knowing the library's role and understanding community needs, librarians are guided by the library's mission and strategic plan, which help to chart the course for determining the work of the library—which consists of library services and programs. A mission and plan tell librarians what work they must do to accomplish a library's goals and objectives to meet needs over a period of time. When librarians know what they plan to accomplish, determining which library services and programs to offer is not so difficult.

Key Points

Librarians who understand the library's mission and the needs of the people they serve are equipped to provide effective programs and services. In these times of economic uncertainty, war, cultural shifts, and new innovations, librarians must stay very focused on the library's purpose and community needs to stay on course.

- A librarian's work accomplishes the role or mission of the library by providing effective library programs and services.
- Every library has a unique mission, and every community has specific needs.
- During times of significant societal shifts that impact our field, libraries' roles shift.
- Librarians must respond rapidly to the changing needs of the people they serve by adapting services and programs to meet community needs effectively.
- Library programs and services are not one size fits all.
- Computers, technology, and the Internet are tools that librarians use to help them meet community needs.

The next chapter introduces a process for discovering library programs and services that will meet your community's needs. Chapter 2 covers the first step: clarifying the library's mission, role, or purpose.

References

Doll, Jen. 2013. "Ask a Librarian About the Odd Things Happening at Libraries." *The Atlantic Wire*, January 8. http://www.theatlanticwire.com/entertainment/2013/01/ask-librarian -about-odd-things-happening-libraries/60710/.

Wisner, William H. 2009. "Restore the Noble Purpose of Libraries." *The Christian Science Monitor*, July 17. http://www.csmonitor.com/Commentary/Opinion/2009/0717/p09s01-coop.html.

CHAPTER 2

Clarifying the Library's Role

UNDERSTANDING YOUR LIBRARY'S ROLE, purpose or mission; possessing a solid knowledge about the current needs of the people the library serves; and library planning will help librarians determine needed services and programs. Figure 2.1 illustrates a process for discovering library programs and services that incorporates these components. When you use this approach you will find that discovering the programs and services that people need is not such a difficult task. Follow these steps and it will make perfect sense when it comes to deciding what your library needs to provide, and what you must do to make that happen.

The first step in the process of designing relevant library programs and services is clarifying the library's role or mission. Some say that libraries don't need mission statements—that having a mission statement is an old-fashioned, outdated concept. Some librarians think mission statements don't serve any purpose except to satisfy the requirements of the library board, larger organization, or state library agency. You may have heard from authorities in our field that a library mission statement is strictly a marketing tool. None of this could be further from the truth. In fact, a library mission statement is a major force that guides you in being effective. It reminds you that what you are doing is meeting community needs. When you lose your way, a mission statement helps steer you back in the right direction.

Looking Back on a Brief History of Library Roles

A look back through the history of libraries illustrates how libraries throughout time have had different and changing roles. Regardless of the type of library or the community you

Figure 2.1. Process for Discovering Library Programs and Services.

serve, we can expect the role or purpose of libraries to continue to evolve. History does not stand still, especially in the information field. People change, and their needs change. For libraries to survive, librarians must embrace change and welcome the reality that the role of libraries is in a constant state of flux—as it always has been.

In the beginning, libraries primarily housed written records. The first libraries were warehouses for records written on clay, bones, skins, bamboo, and papyrus. As these materials accumulated in libraries, a need arose to organize them for efficient storage, and for accessing and retrieving them for use by the people the library served. When the need for organizing and cataloging records arose, library workers then became responsible for organizing and cataloging records so people could find them. In time, library workers assumed the roles of collecting, translating, accessing, copying, and protecting written records. As methods for recording written records and for communicating information evolved, librarians adapted by incorporating new innovations to help them accomplish their work and to meet people's needs. Some library roles throughout history include:

- Store written records
- Organize and catalog materials
- Serve as academic communities and centers of knowledge and learning
- Copy, collect, and translate materials
- Show off wealth, status, and social position
- Support the public good
- Encourage reading
- Improve the literacy rate
- Promote self-improvement
- Support adult education
- Support students, faculty, and staff
- Support researchers, or research and development
- Provide recreation and entertainment
- Provide a meeting place
- Support governments

The work of librarians has been influenced by significant innovations in the methods for recording, organizing, and accessing information. The type of library, the nature of the people the library serves, and their particular needs help determine a library's mission or role. For instance, McClure's *Planning and Role-Setting for Public Libraries* (1987) proposes different roles for library planners to consider when defining their library's services:

1. Community activity center
2. Community information center
3. Formal education support center
4. Independent learning center
5. Popular materials library
6. Preschoolers' door to library

Later, Nelson's *The New Planning for Results* (2001) defined thirteen service responses meant to help public library planners link community needs with library services and programs by defining the library's role:

1. Basic library
2. Business and career information
3. Commons
4. Community referral
5. Consumer information
6. Cultural awareness
7. Current topics and titles
8. Formal learning support
9. General information
10. Government information
11. Information literacy
12. Lifelong learning
13. Local history and genealogy

Regardless of the type of library or the population it serves, it is important to remember that the fundamental purpose of a library is to meet people's information needs. A library's role or mission is usually defined within the broad traditional function of libraries to acquire, organize, retrieve, and disseminate information; promote learning; improve literacy; and encourage reading. A mission statement can be simple or functional. It needs to be specific enough to focus library functions; yet it should allow enough room for growth and movement in response to changing communities.

Librarians are in the business of meeting people's information needs.

◎ Understanding Your Library's Role, Purpose, or Mission

What is your library's role? Is it to encourage reading among young people? Improve the literacy rate? Help people lead productive lives? Serve as a meeting place? Provide a safe haven for teens after school? Promote adult education? Support the curriculum in a school? Provide a space for college students to study and learn? Or provide collaborative workspaces for researchers in a corporate environment?

A library's role is articulated in its mission statement. Library mission statements state why the library exists, and they are tailored to the specific population the library serves. Mission statements inspire librarians, and they help guide libraries through times of significant change and groundbreaking innovations in the information field. During population shifts or decreased library funding, mission statements will show you the way. They will guide you when you are unsure about the right direction. Mission statements will tell you what you need to do next, and they will inspire you in your day-to-day work.

Balas aptly states, "Libraries are suffering from an identity crisis" (2007, 30). Libraries are not just about books any more. Because they now have different media, computers, and the Internet, libraries have diversified. But what have libraries diversified into? And how do librarians decide which way to go when they diversify their libraries? Some libraries now serve as community centers, entertainment centers, or social centers with cafés, gaming activity centers, and recreational facilities that also happen to provide traditional information resources.

Metcalfe (2013) writes about a design for a proposed new library in Mosina, Poland, where the books are located on the first floor. On the next level, "there is a glass column full of water and flailing human bodies," and on another level "you're suddenly in the middle of a vast swimming facility, complete with a snaking water slide that takes whooping swimmers on a ride inside and outside the building." Surveys showed that 56 percent of Poles had not read a book in the past year and that they were not interested in building new libraries. So the architect, Hugon Kowalski, designed this mixed-use library as a way to attract Poles who are really more interested in sports and recreational facilities, pools and retail shops. What is the library's core purpose or mission? Is it to fulfill the recreational and entertainment needs of the people, even when those needs have nothing to do with information, knowledge, or learning? What is the relationship between the library attractions and poor reading habits?

When librarians know their library's role, they can focus on fulfilling the mission. It will be clear to them which way to go when a difficult decision is to be made. If a board member proposes to place a pool table in the reading room, librarians must refer to the mission statement, asking how the pool table helps to do the library's work or to enhance the reading room. This is not to say that it won't; it is only to say that as librarians we must ask this question before we diversify. We need to be clear about how the pool table will contribute to the work of the library. This is the same process we ask ourselves when we consider providing a new service or program, or implementing new technology.

Librarians who are confident about their library's role and how their work relates to it are focused. They are less likely to become distracted by diversification itself or by purchasing new technology because it is trendy. Librarians who are inspired by the library's mission are motivated to provide specific programs and services that will meet people's information needs. They are motivated to make a difference in people's lives by actualizing the library's mission through their work. Librarians who are guided by the library's mission are clear about which technologies will help them implement appropriate and successful new programs and services. They know why they are doing what they are doing. They are less likely to be lured by flashy new products and slick salespeople.

Mission statements are also very useful when it comes to telling customers or users about what the library strives to do. When a library is part of a larger organization such as a university, business, law office, school district, or municipality, the library's mission statement aligns the library with the mission of the larger organization to ensure that the library and the organization are proceeding in the same direction. Being clear about the library's mission can be very helpful when you are advocating for the library or justifying continued or additional funding for needed programs and services; however, these are some positive effects of having a mission statement, not reasons for having one.

MISSION STATEMENT EXERCISE

Using the library's mission statement as your only resource, complete the following exercise.

1. Write your library's mission statement.

   _____
   _____
   _____

2. What does the mission statement say about why the library exists?

   _____
   _____
   _____
   _____

3. How does the mission statement speak to the specific population your library serves?

   _____
   _____
   _____
   _____

4. What does the mission statement say about library programs and services?

   _____
   _____
   _____
   _____

5. How does the mission statement inspire you? How does it help guide you through difficult or challenging times for the library?

   _____
   _____
   _____
   _____

6. What does the mission statement say to customers or users about what the library does?

   _____
   _____
   _____
   _____

7. How does the mission statement relate to the larger organization?

   _____
   _____
   _____
   _____

If the Mission Statement Exercise was a challenge for you, or if your library's mission statement didn't address many of these questions, look at the mission statement examples below. Use them to help you write or revise your library's mission statement. The first five examples are from various organizations that are NOT libraries. How do they resemble your library's mission statement? How are they different from your library's mission statement? Do you see an idea, concept, or approach in one or several of them that could enhance your library's mission statement?

NONLIBRARY MISSION STATEMENT EXAMPLES

Starbucks

To inspire and nurture the human spirit—one person, one cup, and one neighborhood at a time. http://www.starbucks.com/about-us/company-information/mission-statement.

St. Jude Children's Research Hospital

To advance cures, and means of prevention, for pediatric catastrophic diseases through research and treatment. Consistent with the vision of our founder, Danny Thomas, no child is denied treatment based on race, religion, or a family's ability to pay. https://www.stjude.org/stjude/v/index.jsp?vgnextoid=9dc4b8ca05604 210VgnVCM1000001e0215acRCRD&vgnextchannel=f67c1e3d40419210Vgn VCM1000001e0215acRCRD.

Dartmouth College

Dartmouth College educates the most promising students and prepares them for a lifetime of learning and of responsible leadership, through a faculty dedicated to teaching and the creation of knowledge. http://www.dartmouth.edu/home/about/mission.html.

Peabody Essex Museum

To celebrate outstanding artistic and cultural creativity by collecting, stewarding, and interpreting objects of art and culture in ways that increase knowledge, enrich the spirit, engage the mind, and stimulate the senses. Through its exhibitions, programs, publications, media, and related activities, PEM strives to create experiences that transform people's lives by broadening their perspectives, attitudes, and knowledge of themselves and the wider world. http://www.pem.org/about/mission_vision.

Intel Corporation

Delight our customers, employees, and shareholders by relentlessly delivering the platform and technology advancements that become essential to the way we work and live. http://www.intel.com/intel/company/corp1.htm#anchor1.

The next five examples are library mission statements. Imagine working in these libraries. Which mission statements are more useful for library staff in clarifying decisions about what services and programs to offer? Which ones are more specific to the people the library serves? Which are less specific or more vague?

LIBRARY MISSION STATEMENT EXAMPLES

San Francisco Public Library, San Francisco. The San Francisco Public Library system is dedicated to free and equal access to information, knowledge, independent learning, and the joys of reading for our diverse community. http://sfpl.org/index.php?pg=2000006901.

Kraemer Family Library, University of Colorado, Colorado Springs. The Kraemer Family Library fosters the intellectual growth of UCCS students, faculty, staff, and our community by developing innovative services, technologies, collections, and spaces that facilitate their emerging information needs. http://www.uccs.edu/library/info/mission.html.

Little Falls Public Library, Little Falls, New York. The mission of the Little Falls Public Library is to be your local connection to a world of information. http://www.lflibrary.org/library-information-history-2/library-mission-statement/.

Appellate Division, Fourth Department Law Library, Rochester, New York. The mission of the law library is to provide legal information to the appellate division, to the Rochester metropolitan region, and to the entire legal community of the Fifth, Seventh, and Eighth Judicial Districts. Our role is unique as the only appellate-level court library in New York state that serves both an active judiciary and practicing bar, and is also open to the general public. Through our services, the library strives to be one of the best court libraries in the nation. http://nycourts gov/library/ad4/library_information/mission.shtml

Conaton Library Media Center, Cathedral High School Library, Indianapolis. The mission of the Cathedral High School Library is to encourage and support students and staff in their quests for knowledge and good books, to provide access to resources to meet their needs, and to help develop the information literacy skills necessary for lifelong reading and independent learning. http://www.cathedral -irish.org/page.cfm?p=26.

Most libraries make their mission statements available to the public on the web. Take time to look at mission statements of libraries similar to yours. How are their mission statements similar to or different from yours? Make notes about how your library's mission statement could be improved based on your observations from examining the mission statements in this chapter, on the web, and in libraries like yours. What can you do to make your library's mission statement more relevant for the community and more useful in your work?

If you find that your library's mission is out of date, or if you have difficulty relating it to the services and programs your library offers, this only means the mission statement needs updating or revisiting. If library staff continuously loses focus about the library's purpose, or if they are unfamiliar with the library's mission, look at the mission statement. If they are not sure why they are doing what they are doing, they have probably lost their way. Librarians may have lost any connection with the meaning of the mission. You can't move forward in defining programs and services without a clear sense of purpose or connection with the mission. If the mission statement is meaningless, too vague, or outdated, no one knows how to decide which programs or services are needed to fulfill the mission.

When no one in a leadership position makes an effort to inform staff what the mission is and that it is the core of everything they do, you may lose your way. Your library may have lost a sense of purpose. When librarians are confused about what programs and services people need or how to determine them, it is usually because the library's mission is not guiding them. Librarians who are not guided by their library's mission may eventually find themselves uninspired by library work or offering the same programs and services for decades. These librarians may try to replicate programs or services that succeeded in other libraries in an effort to find their way. Other librarians who offer programs and services that they somehow "know" intuitively are effective will discover one day that the services and programs they have been offering for decades are irrelevant. In time, libraries like this atrophy.

⌾ Key Points

If your library's mission statement was written thirty years ago and library staff does not even know what it is, the work of your library is probably not relevant. If your library director filled in a generic mission statement template or repurposed a mission statement from another library, your library does not have the interests of the people you serve as a priority. Write a mission statement that means something to the community and the people you serve.

- The first step in the process of designing relevant library programs and services begins with clarifying the library's role or mission.
- A mission statement is a major force that guides you in being effective.
- The work of librarians has been influenced by significant innovations in the methods for recording, organizing, and accessing information.
- Regardless of the type of library or the population it serves, the fundamental purpose of a library is to meet people's information needs.
- We can expect the role or purpose of libraries to continue to evolve.
- Mission statements inspire librarians and help guide libraries through times of significant change and groundbreaking innovations in the information field.
- The library's mission statement aligns the library with the mission of the larger organization.
- Without a purpose or connection to community needs, you can't define programs and services.

The next step in the process is creating a community profile. Chapter 3 explains how to understand the overall nature of your community by finding and compiling existing data. The community profile will inform the community needs assessment process.

◎ References

Balas, Janet L. 2007. "Do You Know What Your Mission Is?" *Computers in Libraries* 27, no. 2 (February): 30–32.

McClure, Charles R. 1987. *Planning and Role-Setting for Public Libraries: A Manual of Options and Procedures.* Chicago: American Library Association.

Metcalfe, John. 2013. "Would More People Use the Public Library If It Had a Water Slide?" *The Atlantic Cities*, March 19. http://www.theatlanticcities.com/design/2013/03/would-more -people-use-public-library-if-it-had-water-slide/5019/.

Nelson, Sandra S. 2001. *New Planning for Results: A Streamlined Approach.* Chicago: American Library Association.

Creating a Community Profile

NOW THAT YOU HAVE CLARIFIED YOUR LIBRARY'S ROLE OR MISSION, the next step is to find out what the people you serve need. This is not necessarily a linear process, because as you know your library's mission statement is shaped by people's needs. In practice you may want to look at the community and people's needs before you write a mission statement. If your mission statement is in place and working well, you may want to look at the community for the purpose of making adjustments to the mission statement.

Once the mission statement, needs assessment, and plans are in place, you will find that the interplay is ongoing among all the elements of the process. For instance, if the population you serve changes significantly, you may want to conduct a community needs assessment, then possibly adjust your mission statement. When your community changes, you will need to update your strategic plan and thus the programs and services you offer. Figure 3.1 illustrates this way of visualizing the process of discovering library services and programs as you will likely experience it once you have your library's mission, needs assessment, and plans in place. The process is presented here in sequential steps to make it easier for readers to understand the basic concepts. Thereafter, you will be able to take the steps when you need to take them, in any order.

Defining Effective Needs Assessments

Before you can offer library services and programs that people need, you must find out what they need. This is obvious; however, many librarians don't assess community needs

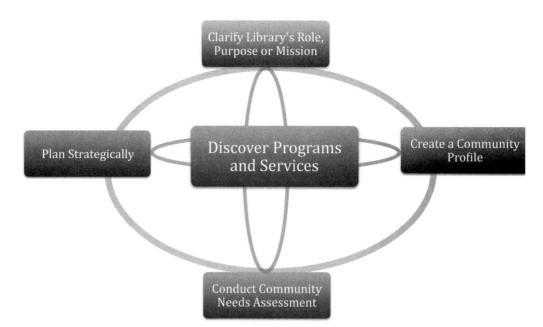

Figure 3.1. Discovering Library Services and Programs in Action.

prior to planning. Needs assessments determine what people need in a community, school, corporation, or college. They use existing data and results and analysis of surveys, questionnaires, interviews, observations, and focus groups, for example, about people in the community and surrounding areas. Needs assessments are typically conducted prior to strategic planning to inform the planning process. This is because planning teams must know the current needs and conditions in a community, school, university, or business to be able to plan effective library services and programs for the people in them.

Providing library programs and services based on outdated data or inaccurate information about people's needs makes no sense. Nor does providing library services and programs that are not designed to meet everyone's needs. Guessing or "knowing" intuitively what people need is an unacceptable assessment method. Thoroughly assessing community needs involves 1) compiling existing data about them and 2) conducting a comprehensive needs assessment.

It is important to include the entire population when you are assessing needs. Your entire population might be everyone living in the community; all faculty, students, and staff in the school; all lawyers, legal staff, and employees in the law firm; or all students, faculty, staff, and researchers in the university, for example. It is essential to understand that the population you serve is not limited to library users. When you are assessing community needs, asking library users what they need or like is an invalid technique, because it excludes people who don't use the library. Unless 100 percent of the people in your community, school, university, or corporation use the library, library users are only a fraction of everyone you serve. Figure 3.2 illustrates this point.

The Pew Report "Library Services in the Digital Age" (Zickuhr, Rainie, and Purcell 2013) found that 59 percent of Americans age sixteen and older had at least one interaction (in person or electronically) with their public library in the past twelve months. This means that 41 percent of Americans age sixteen and older had *no* interaction with their public libraries in the past twelve months. The report is revealing about who uses libraries, how they use them, what they would like in a library, and what kinds of information they access through libraries and the information-seeking habits of different population

Figure 3.2. Community versus Library Users.

segments. Librarians are very good at analyzing library users; however, sometimes they forget that libraries don't just serve the people who use them. It is the library's work to serve everyone within a defined population. Focusing on users alone while ignoring everyone else is not an option.

A survey of library users asking them how they like the library is not a community needs assessment: It is a customer satisfaction survey. If you have been distributing customer satisfaction surveys to library users, this is a good thing to do periodically, but it is not a community needs assessment. Also, a library needs assessment—or list of things the library needs—cannot be substituted for an assessment of people's needs. Community needs assessments are people focused, not library focused. You can determine what the library needs only after you find out what people need and then design programs and services to meet their needs. What the library lacks to provide effective programs and services determines what the library needs.

The value of a library is diminished when its programs and services have little or nothing to do with the needs of the people in an entire community. People will not visit a library that doesn't meet their needs. Furthermore, out-of-touch libraries are in danger of losing funding because they are irrelevant.

◎ Defining a Community Profile

A first step in discovering what the people you serve need is to create a community profile. Community profiles contain information about your community—school, college, or university; law office, hospital, or corporation—as well as the characteristics of the people who live, teach, or work there. For instance, for public libraries this usually means a city, village, county, or other geographic area and the people who live there; for corporate libraries, this usually means the corporation and employees; for school libraries, the school or school district and students, teachers, and administration; and for academic libraries, a college or university and students, faculty, researchers, and staff. For school, academic, and special libraries, community profiles may also contain information about the surrounding geographic area where the school, academic institution, or special library exists. This could be a town, city, or county, for instance.

A community profile will help you design appropriate assessment methodologies and design relevant questionnaires, surveys, or other assessment instruments. It will reveal other programs and services in your community that are meeting similar needs, and it will show you other departments, agencies, and businesses that are potential partners in planning and implementing future library programs and services. A community profile will also help identify stakeholders for library planning.

◎ Gathering and Compiling Data

Gathering and compiling existing information about the people you serve and the environment where they work, attend school, or reside provides a solid foundation that will inform a needs assessment and may reveal some current information needs. Look for a broad range of information, and pay special attention to any data that indicate an information need. Think about how the data and information might translate into an information need. Take notes and record information as you find it on the Community Profile Worksheet below. Use additional paper if you need it and bookmark any websites you use as resources in a folder named "Community Profile."

COMMUNITY PROFILE WORKSHEET

Use this worksheet to record information and data about your library and the people it serves, as well as your organization and the surrounding community. Make notes about the source(s) where you found the information.

1. Who does your library serve? For example, all of the people in your municipality; all of the faculty, students, and staff at your college; all of the employees in your department, agency, or organization; or all of the teachers and students at your school?

   _____

   _____

   _____

   _____

---

2. How many people does your library serve? Give a total and also break down each segment, if applicable. For example, for school libraries, record the number of students as well as the number of teachers; academic libraries: record number of faculty, staff, students, and researchers separately; hospital libraries: record the number of medical staff and the number of patients. Public libraries: record the number of people in the city, town, county, or region your library serves.

_____

_____

_____

_____

3. What are the demographics for each segment you listed above? For example, what are their age groups; what are their income levels; education levels; ethnic groups; medical or legal specialties; test scores; positions or jobs; unemployment rates; grade levels; cumulative grade averages; ethnic backgrounds; or first languages?

_____

_____

_____

_____

4. Where are they? For example, do they all live, work, or attend school in one physical location, or are they in multiple locations such as corporate offices all over the world; main and branch college campuses; or multiple schools in a school district? Are there remote users in multiple locations? Where?

_____

_____

_____

_____

5. What are the population trends? For example, are people leaving, or is the population you serve reducing? Are there increasingly more young people? Older people? Are education levels shifting? Income levels? Is there an influx of new immigrants? Where are people moving in from? What areas are new people moving into? What positions are they filling? Does the population increase in the summer? Winter?

_____

_____

_____

_____

6. If you are a school, special, or academic librarian, describe the characteristics of the surrounding town, village, city, county, and/or state where your library is situated. What are the demographics and population trends of the community where the school, corporation, or university exists?

_____

_____

_____

7. For all library types: List the major industries and largest employers in your surrounding community. How many people do they employ? Are there any trends over the past ten years? Downsizing and layoffs? New plants opening?

_____
_____
_____

8. List nearby businesses.

_____
_____
_____

9. List the social services agencies in your community.

_____
_____
_____

10. List other services and programs in your community. For example, city recreational services and programs, university tutoring programs, prison GED programs, ESL programs, after school programs, or literacy programs?

_____
_____
_____

11. List the schools in your community and their grade levels.

_____
_____
_____

12. List other nearby libraries.

_____
_____
_____

13. Where do people get their information in your community?

_____
_____
_____
_____

Begin by accessing data that have already been compiled and prepared within your own organization. You can find a great deal of information about your community, school, college, or corporation from resources that are readily available to you, for example:

- U.S. Census Bureau
- State and local studies

- Government and private data and reports
- Foundation reports
- Assessments or studies by other organizations
- Corporate headquarters
- Corporate reports
- Human resources office
- School administrations, school district offices
- University research office or grants office
- City hall, village offices, town administration
- County and city data book
- Community grants agencies
- City planning office
- American demographics
- Community services directories
- Newspapers or local periodicals

What other kinds of things could you look at to define your community? Here are a few:

- Economic, social, and political trends
- History
- Relationship with surrounding communities
- Technological familiarity
- Trends or changing community conditions

Look around. What are people in your community doing? Where do they gather? What kinds of businesses are there? What cultural opportunities are there? What languages are spoken? What schools are there? What kinds of residential units? Talk to people. Ask other agencies what they are providing. What needs do they see? Talk to librarians in other nearby libraries about any needs they see.

It is not unusual for communities to change drastically in very short periods of time. Unless librarians make it their business to stay abreast of new developments in their communities, including new and emerging needs, those needs will likely go unmet. To meet new needs and stay relevant, you must stay informed about your community. For example, if a large immigrant population has relocated to your community over the past year, it could be that suddenly a high number of people there do not speak English. If you are unaware of this, chances are very high that the library is not providing programs and services that meet the information needs of these new residents. When you create a community profile, you will discover changes among the people you serve that will help you provide more effective programs and services for your entire population. Make sure to check the dates on any assessments that you use as sources.

Some communities, schools, colleges, universities, states, cities, counties, and corporations have already created community profiles you can use. Check websites for the labor, commerce, economic, and tourism bureaus and offices in your area for information about your community or surrounding communities. Some state websites where you might find your community profile or information to include in your community profile are:

The Illinois Department of Commerce and Economic Opportunity (http://www2 .locationone.com/(S(24durglkcuwavedjsxtciqda))/StateMainPage.aspx?source= handler&type=state&profileid=IL-DCCA&appsection=community) offers community profiles for Illinois counties, metro regions, and localities in Illinois.

Virginia Labor Market Information (http://data.virginialmi.com/gsipub/index .asp?docid=342) offers complete community profiles for counties and cities in Virginia.

New Hampshire Economic & Labor Market Information Bureau (http://www .nhes.nh.gov/elmi/products/cp/) offers community profiles for communities and counties in New Hampshire (see figure 3.3).

STATS Indiana (http://www.stats.indiana.edu/profiles/profiles.asp?scope_choice=a& county_changer=1800) provides statistics for counties throughout Indiana and more.

The U.S. Census Bureau provides information it has collected, compiled, and organized at these websites:

QuickFacts provides summary profiles using frequently requested data for states, counties, and cities (http://quickfacts.census.gov/qfd/index.html) (see figure 3.4).

Census Flows Mapper shows migration flows to and from your county (http:// flowsmapper.geo.census.gov/flowsmapper/map.html).

American FactFinder (http://factfinder.census.gov/faces/nav/jsf/pages/index.xhtml) provides popular facts and frequently requested data about communities. The advanced search allows you to search and sort data to your specifications (see figure 3.5).

Public librarians can usually find what they need for community profiles using resources such as those listed above; however, special librarians generally serve a smaller and more contained population. Gathering data about the corporation or business, law firm, hospital, or prison where the library is situated is sometimes an easier task than gathering information about an entire community. A special library is likely a repository for information about the business or corporation, its history and trends. Check with the human resources office for more detailed information about current employees. Corporations and businesses usually produce annual reports that are full of useful information you can use to create a profile. If your corporate library also serves the surrounding community, include data about the community in your profile.

Schools, colleges, and universities are well known for tracking and keeping extensive statistics about their populations. Check in your school or school district's administrative offices or with your state education department for information. For example, the Massachusetts Department of Elementary and Secondary Education's

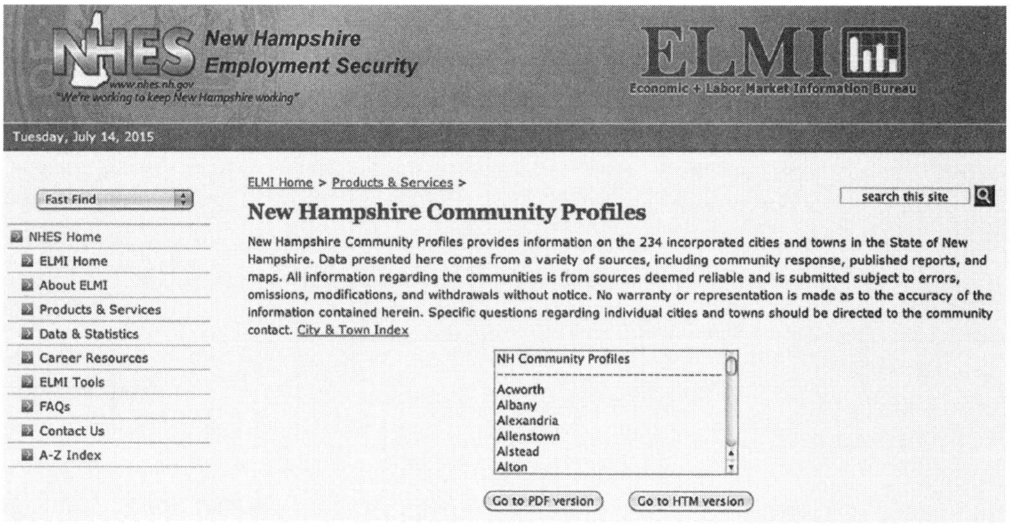

Figure 3.3. New Hampshire Economic and Labor Market Information Bureau.

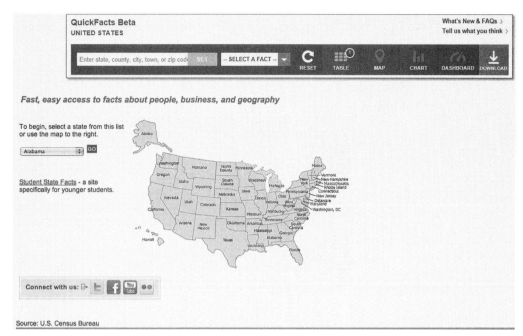

Source: U.S. Census Bureau

Figure 3.4. QuickFacts.

website (http://profiles.doe.mass.edu/) provides data from schools and districts across the state that is searchable by multiple fields (see figure 3.6). The National Center for Education Statistics' Data Tools page (http://nces.ed.gov/datatools/index.asp?Data-ToolSectionID=4) offers numerous ways to build custom tables by state, school district, or school (see figure 3.7). This database makes available multiple data sets such as test results, finance, enrollment, human resources, and student achievement in different disciplines such as financial literacy.

Figure 3.5. American FactFinder.

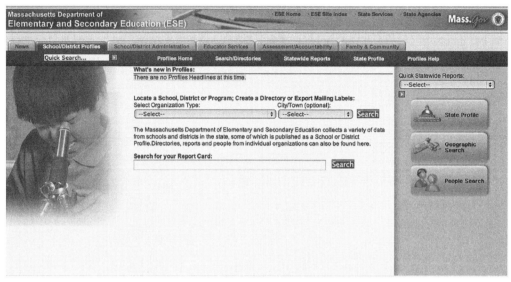

Figure 3.6. Massachusetts Department of Elementary and Secondary Education.

Use your information searching skills to find needs assessment results or other studies that may have been conducted by other agencies in your state or area. For example, in New Mexico, the Bureau of Business and Economic Research at the University of New Mexico (http://bber.unm.edu/pubscommunity.htm) makes many of its studies and community assessments available to the public on the web (see figure 3.8).

:ies INSTITUTE OF EDUCATION SCIENCES

NATIONAL CENTER FOR **EDUCATION STATISTICS**

Enter search terms here

Publications & Products | Surveys & Programs | Data & Tools | Fast Facts | School Search | News & Events | About Us

🛠 DATA TOOLS

Education Data Analysis Tool (EDAT)

Download NCES survey datasets in various statistical software formats. Customize your dataset by selecting a survey, population, and variables relevant to your research analysis.
Visit Education Data Analysis Tool (EDAT)

Elementary/Secondary Information System (ELSi)

View public and private school data and create custom tables using ELSi—a quick and easy tool for obtaining basic statistical data using the most common variables and tables from CCD and PSS.
Visit Elementary/Secondary Information System (ELSi)

International Data Explorer (IDE)

This tool provides you with tables of detailed results from the International Assessments. The data are based on information gathered from the students, teachers, and schools that participated in PISA, PIRLS, and TIMSS. The IDE provides results for the United States and other jurisdictions around the world from the administration of these assessments.
Visit International Data Explorer (IDE)

IPEDS Analytics: Delta Cost Project Database

Download a longitudinal database derived from IPEDS finance, enrollment, human resources, completions, graduation rates and student financial aid data for academic years 1986-87 through 2009-10. These data have been translated into analytical formats to allow for longitudinal analyses of trends in postsecondary education with a focus on revenues and expenditures.
Visit IPEDS Analytics: Delta Cost Project Database

National Assessment of Educational Progress (NAEP) Data Explorer

This tool provides you with tables of detailed results from NAEP's national and state assessments. The data are based on information gathered from the students, teachers, and schools that participated in NAEP.
Visit National Assessment of Educational Progress (NAEP) Data Explorer

Figure 3.7. National Center for Education Statistics' Data Tools.

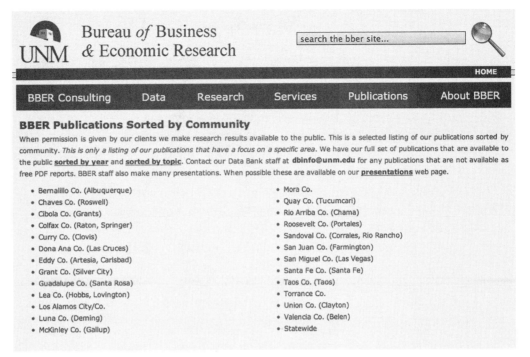

Figure 3.8. UNM Bureau of Business and Economic Research.

Locate the economic or business research center in an academic institution close to you. Search its website or contact it by phone if you cannot find or access the information you need.

Search specialized databases for more specific information about people's needs. For instance, for detailed information about children, the Kids Count Data Center (http://data center.kidscount.org/) maintained by the Annie E. Casey Foundation compiles information about children regarding education, economic well-being, family and community, health, safety, and risky behaviors. The database is searchable by geographic region or data topic.

Compile the information and data you gathered into a community profile that is customized for your community and library. This must be easy to read and interpret. Manchester, New Hampshire, for example, has a community profile that is thorough and easy to use (see figures 3.9a, 3.9b, and 3.9c). It contains more information than you will need for the library's assessment. Use what is relevant. As you write your own community's profile, eliminate jargon, clarify acronyms, and convert shorthand notes into complete phrases or sentences. You will use this community profile for planning purposes, which means that other people must be able to use it.

The community profile will inform the community needs assessment you will conduct next (see chapter 4). For instance, your community profile may reveal that the students in your school are performing poorly in writing, or that the people in your community are primarily non-English speakers. This knowledge will help you focus on areas where the library can help solve problems. Remember to update the community profile as new and relevant information and data emerge. This is important to keep your programs and services relevant.

Manchester, NH

Community Contact	Manchester Economic Development Office
	William Craig, Director
	One City Hall Plaza, Suite 110
	Manchester, NH 03101-2099
Telephone	(603) 624-6505
Fax	(603) 624-6308
E-mail	econdev@manchesternh.gov
Web Site	www.ManchesterNH.gov
Municipal Office Hours	Monday through Friday, 8 am - 5 pm
County	Hillsborough
Labor Market Area	Manchester, NH Metropolitan NECTA
Tourism Region	Merrimack Valley
Planning Commission	Southern NH
Regional Development	Capital Regional Development Council
Election Districts	
US Congress	District 1 (All Wards)
Executive Council	District 4 (All Wards)
State Senate	District 16 (Wards 1, 2, & 12), 18 (Wards 5-9), and 20 (Wards 3, 4, 10, & 11)
State Representative	Hillsborough County Districts 8, 42 (Ward 1) 9, 42 (Ward 2) 10, 42 (Ward 3) 11, 43 (Ward 4) 12, 43 (Ward 5) 13, 43 (Ward 6) 14, 43 (Ward 7) 15, 44 (Ward 8) 16, 44 (Ward 9) 17, 45 (Ward 10) 18, 45 (Ward 11) 19, 45 (Ward 12)

Incorporated: 1751

Origin: This territory, first known as Harrytown, was granted in 1735 as Tyng's Town to Captain William Tyng's "snow-shoe men" who had fought in the French and Indian War during the winter of 1703. In 1751, it was incorporated as Derryfield, and included part of Chester and Londonderry. The name Manchester was suggested by Samuel Blodgett, a businessman who found that the Amoskeag Falls impeded shipping on the Merrimack River. He had visited Manchester, England, and was determined to build a canal like those in England. The canal was opened in May 1807, and though Mr. Blodgett died later that year, the town was renamed Manchester in 1810. The first cotton spinning mill opened in 1804, and the Amoskeag Cotton and Wool Manufacturing Company opened in 1810. Manchester was incorporated as a city in 1846.

Hillsborough County

Villages and Place Names: Goffs Falls, Massabesic, Youngsville, Bakersville, Amoskeag

Population, Year of the First Census Taken: 362 residents in 1790

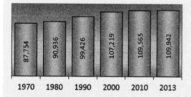

1970	1980	1990	2000	2010	2013
87,754	90,936	99,426	107,219	109,565	109,942

Population Trends: The state's largest city, population change for Manchester was the fifth largest, totaling 21,660 over 53 years, from 88,282 in 1960 to 109,942 in 2013. The largest decennial percent change was just nine percent, between 1980 and 1990. The 2013 Census estimate for Manchester was 109,942 residents, which ranked first among New Hampshire's incorporated cities and towns.

Population Density and Land Area, 2013 *(US Census Bureau)*: 3,326.5 persons per square mile of land area, the state's highest population density. Manchester contains 33.1 square miles of land area and 1.9 square miles of inland water area.

Economic & Labor Market Information Bureau, NH Employment Security, March 2015. Community Response Received 7/11/2014

Figure 3.9a. Manchester, NH, Community Profile—Page 1.

MUNICIPAL SERVICES

Type of Government	Mayor & 14 Aldermen
Budget: Municipal Appropriations, 2014-2015	$159,562,680
Budget: School Appropriations, 2014-2015	$143,773,080
Zoning Ordinance	1927/12
Master Plan	2010
Capital Improvement Plan	Yes
Industrial Plans Reviewed By	City Planning Board

Boards and Commissions
Elected: Mayor; Aldermen; School
Appointed: Planning; Conservation; Zoning; Library; 25 others

Public Library   Manchester City; West Side Community

EMERGENCY SERVICES

Police Department	Full-time
Fire Department	Municipal
Emergency Medical Service	Municipal

Nearest Hospital(s)	Distance	Staffed Beds
Elliot Hospital, Manchester	Local	279
Catholic Medical Center, Manchester	Local	233

UTILITIES

Electric Supplier	Eversource Energy
Natural Gas Supplier	Liberty Utilities
Water Supplier	Manchester Water Works
Sanitation	Municipal
Municipal Wastewater Treatment Plant	Yes
Solid Waste Disposal	
Curbside Trash Pickup	Municipal
Pay-As-You-Throw Program	No
Recycling Program	Yard waste-Mandatory; Recyclables-Voluntary
Telephone Company	Fairpoint
Cellular Telephone Access	Yes
Cable Television Access	Yes
Public Access Television Station	Yes
High Speed Internet Service: Business	Yes
Residential	Yes

PROPERTY TAXES (NH Dept. of Revenue Administration)

2013 Total Tax Rate (per $1000 of value)	$22.67
2013 Equalization Ratio	101.0
2013 Full Value Tax Rate (per $1000 of value)	$22.33

2013 Percent of Local Assessed Valuation by Property Type

Residential Land and Buildings	62.3%
Commercial Land and Buildings	35.0%
Public Utilities, Current Use, and Other	2.7%

HOUSING (ACS 2009-2013)

Total Housing Units	49,025
Single-Family Units, Detached or Attached	20,904
Units in Multiple-Family Structures:	
Two to Four Units in Structure	13,301
Five or More Units in Structure	14,684
Mobile Homes and Other Housing Units	136

DEMOGRAPHICS (US Census Bureau)

Total Population	Community	County
2013	109,942	402,979
2010	109,565	400,721
2000	107,219	382,384
1990	99,426	336,549
1980	90,936	276,608
1970	87,754	223,941

Demographics, American Community Survey (ACS) 2009-2013

Population by Gender

Male	55,013	Female	54,929

Population by Age Group

Under age 5	6,755
Age 5 to 19	19,266
Age 20 to 34	26,959
Age 35 to 54	30,539
Age 55 to 64	12,707
Age 65 and over	13,716
Median Age	36.1 years

Educational Attainment, population 25 years and over

High school graduate or higher	86.7%
Bachelor's degree or higher	26.0%

INCOME, INFLATION ADJUSTED $ (ACS 2009-2013)

Per capita income	$28,055
Median family income	$65,892
Median household income	$54,496
Median Earnings, full-time, year-round workers	
Male	$47,322
Female	$38,424
Individuals below the poverty level	14.2%

LABOR FORCE (NHES – ELMI)

Annual Average	2003	2013
Civilian labor force	60,569	62,336
Employed	57,749	58,862
Unemployed	2,820	3,474
Unemployment rate	4.7%	5.6%

EMPLOYMENT & WAGES (NHES – ELMI)

Annual Average Covered Employment	2003	2013
Goods Producing Industries		
Average Employment	9,539	7,279
Average Weekly Wage	$ 833	$1,139
Service Providing Industries		
Average Employment	49,318	51,237
Average Weekly Wage	$ 741	$ 969
Total Private Industry		
Average Employment	58,857	58,516
Average Weekly Wage	$ 756	$ 990
Government (Federal, State, and Local)		
Average Employment	7,888	6,887
Average Weekly Wage	$ 811	$1,123
Total, Private Industry plus Government		
Average Employment	66,746	65,403
Average Weekly Wage	$ 763	$1,003

Economic & Labor Market Information Bureau, NH Employment Security, March 2015. Community Response Received 7/11/2014

Figure 3.9b.   Manchester, NH, Community Profile—Page 2.

EDUCATION AND CHILD CARE

Schools students attend: **Manchester operates grades K-12**   District: **SAU 37**
Career Technology Center(s): **Manchester School of Technology**   Region: **15**

Educational Facilities (includes Charter Schools)	Elementary	Middle/Junior High	High School	Private/Parochial
Number of Schools	16	6	6	13
Grade Levels	P K 1-6	6-8	9-12	P K 1-12
Total Enrollment	7,051	3,076	4,887	2,092

Nearest Community College: **Manchester**
Nearest Colleges or Universities: **Hesser; St. Anselm; Southern NH University; UNH-Manchester**

2014 NH Licensed Child Care Facilities (DHHS-Bureau of Child Care Licensing)   Total Facilities: **57** Total Capacity: **4,548**

LARGEST BUSINESSES	PRODUCT/SERVICE	EMPLOYEES	ESTABLISHED
Elliot Hospital	Health care services	3,375	
Catholic Medical Center	Health care services	2,100	
Eversource Energy	Utility	1,500	
Fairpoint Communications	Utility	1,300	
TD Bank	Banking services	1,100	
Comcast	Utility	1,025	
Southern NH University	Education	1,000	
Citizens Bank	Banking services	1,000	
Saint Anselm College	Education	663	
Anthem Blue Cross & Blue Shield	Health insurance services	650	

TRANSPORTATION (distances estimated from city/town hall)

Road Access	US Routes	3
	State Routes	3A, 28, 28A 101, 114, 114A
Nearest Interstate, Exit		I-93, Exits 6 - 8; I-293, Exits 1 - 7
	Distance	Local access
Railroad		Guilford Rail Service
Public Transportation		MTA

Nearest Public Use Airport, General Aviation
Manchester-Boston Regional   Runway   9,250 ft. asphalt
Lighted? **Yes**   Navigation Aids?   **Yes**

Nearest Airport with Scheduled Service
Manchester-Boston Regional   Distance   Local
Number of Passenger Airlines Serving Airport   4

Driving distance to select cities:
Manchester, NH	0 miles
Portland, Maine	95 miles
Boston, Mass.	53 miles
New York City, NY	253 miles
Montreal, Quebec	259 miles

COMMUTING TO WORK   (ACS 2009-2013)

Workers 16 years and over	
Drove alone, car/truck/van	81.7%
Carpooled, car/truck/van	9.7%
Public transportation	1.7%
Walked	2.4%
Other means	0.8%
Worked at home	3.8%
Mean Travel Time to Work	25.2 minutes

Percent of Working Residents: ACS 2009-2013
Working in community of residence	42.5
Commuting to another NH community	29.0
Commuting out-of-state	28.5

RECREATION, ATTRACTIONS, AND EVENTS

X	Municipal Parks
X	YMCA/YWCA
X	Boys Club/Girls Club
X	Golf Courses
X	Swimming: Indoor Facility
X	Swimming: Outdoor Facility
X	Tennis Courts: Indoor Facility
X	Tennis Courts: Outdoor Facility
X	Ice Skating Rink: Indoor Facility
X	Bowling Facilities
X	Museums
X	Cinemas
X	Performing Arts Facilities
X	Tourist Attractions
X	Youth Organizations (i.e., Scouts, 4-H)
X	Youth Sports: Baseball
X	Youth Sports: Soccer
X	Youth Sports: Football
X	Youth Sports: Basketball
X	Youth Sports: Hockey
	Campgrounds
X	Fishing/Hunting
X	Boating/Marinas
X	Snowmobile Trails
X	Bicycle Trails
X	Cross Country Skiing
X	Beach or Waterfront Recreation Area
	Overnight or Day Camps

Nearest Ski Area(s): **McIntyre**

Other: **Currier Museum of Art; Amoskeag Fishways Learning Center; Verizon Wireless Arena; Palace Theatre; NH Fishercats Baseball; Manchester Monarchs Hockey; SEE Science Center; Millyard Museum; Franco-American Center**

Figure 3.9c.   Manchester, NH, Community Profile—Page 3.

⊚ Key Points

A library mission statement and a community profile give you the information you need to plan and conduct a community needs assessment. When you know your community and what people need, you will be able to plan effective library programs and services.

- Before you can offer library services and programs that people need, you must find out what they need.
- Needs assessments are typically conducted prior to strategic planning to inform the planning process.
- Needs assessments use existing data and results and analysis of surveys, questionnaires, interviews, observations, and focus groups, for example, about people in the community and surrounding areas.
- Thoroughly assessing community needs involves 1) compiling existing data about them and 2) conducting a comprehensive needs assessment.
- It is important to include the entire population when you are assessing needs.
- Community needs assessments are people focused, not library focused.
- A first step in discovering what the people you serve need is to create a community profile.
- Begin by accessing data that have already been compiled and prepared within your own organization.
- Use your information searching skills to find needs assessment results or other studies that may have been conducted by other agencies in your state or area.
- Some communities; schools, colleges, and universities; states, cities, counties, and corporations have already created community profiles you can use.
- To meet new needs and stay relevant, you must stay informed about your community.

In the next chapter you will learn that a community needs assessment is necessary before you can plan relevant programs and services that make a difference for people. Chapter 4 shows you how to prepare for an assessment and explains the different methodologies you can use to assess community needs.

⊚ Reference

Zickuhr, Kathryn, Lee Rainie, and Kristen Purcell. 2013. *Library Services in the Digital Age.* Washington, DC: Pew Research Center. Internet and American Life Project. http://libraries .pewinternet.org/2013/01/22/library-services.

Assessing Community Needs

IN THIS CHAPTER

▷ Assessing people's needs is essential

▷ Defining communities, community needs, user needs, and library needs

▷ Planning an effective community needs assessment

▷ Understanding community needs assessments

▷ Finding out what people need

▷ Methodologies for assessing needs

▷ Conducting community needs assessments

▷ Compiling data

▷ Preparing and looking ahead

A S DISCUSSED IN CHAPTER 3, the first step in providing needed library services and programs is to know your library's mission or purpose. The next step is to discover people's needs within the parameters of the library's mission. One proven method for doing this is to conduct a community needs assessment, or ask people about their information needs. Once you know people's information needs, you can plan relevant library programs and services, implement them, and evaluate their effectiveness.

Conducting a comprehensive needs assessment takes careful thought and preparation. Needs assessments can be time-consuming and expensive. It is essential to stop and think clearly about what you are doing and why at this point in the process of planning library programs and services. By focusing the needs assessment on aspects of your library's mission or role, you can save time, energy, and money, as well as extract more useful information for future planning.

⊚ Assessing People's Needs Is Essential

Library services and programs must meet the needs of people in your community; school, college, or university; law office, hospital, or corporation—and they must make a difference. Why? If you don't meet people's needs, the library is serving no purpose. People who use the library will eventually stop using it, and those who don't use the library will have no reason to start. The survival of libraries depends on meeting people's needs.

Public and private funding is decreasing, and the funding that is available is not going to continue to flow to libraries just because "everyone loves libraries" or because libraries give people warm and fuzzy feelings. The current economic climate requires that librarians demonstrate the value or return on investment of their libraries to their funding sources. Librarians are being asked to show how the funds they use to offer services and programs provide a good return on the city's, college's, school's, or corporation's investment. The people holding the purse strings want to know how the community is benefiting from the library. It is no longer sufficient to present administrators with spreadsheets showing rising circulation statistics or increasing library visits to demonstrate the library's effectiveness. These days, librarians must meaningfully answer questions such as, "What difference do library programs and services actually make for people?" As funding decreases, accountability for funding increases.

It is not uncommon for some librarians to provide the same programs and services year in and year out without giving it much thought, as long as people are using the library and attending programs. When it comes to technology, "there does not seem to be a conscious and well-defined effort on the part of librarians to identify community computing needs, develop service roles to meet those needs, and implement and administer the activities related to these roles" (McClure and Jaeger 2009, 57). Instead of consciously planning for Internet services and programs to meet demonstrated needs, some librarians seem only to want to "have more" in the way of workstations, bandwidth, databases, and applications (McClure and Jaeger). This clearly is not a sustainable approach.

Librarians are busy people, and admittedly it is no simple task to undertake a comprehensive community needs assessment along with performing all of their other duties. On the other hand, it is impossible to deliver effective programs and services that people need without first assessing their needs. You can conduct needs assessments on a smaller scale that will get you started on the right track.

⊚ Defining Communities, Community Needs, User Needs, and Library Needs

Before you invest time and effort in planning and conducting a needs assessment, it is essential to be clear about what you are doing and why so you can use your time effectively. The terms "community," "community needs," "user needs," "library needs," and "community needs assessment" are interpreted and understood in nearly as many ways as there are librarians who use them. The library science literature is inconsistent in their meaning and use, which sometimes results in confusion among librarians about them. It is necessary to grasp these essential concepts firmly if you are going to conduct an effective assessment that you can use to plan needed library services and programs.

COMMUNITY: all of the people the library serves. For example, all of the people who live in a city, village, or town; all students, staff, faculty, and researchers in a college or university; all students, teachers, administrators, and staff in a school or postsecondary institution; all employees, medical staff, patients, and their families in a hospital; all lawyers, legal assistants, and staff in a law office.

COMMUNITY NEEDS: the needs of all of the people in the community. Librarians are usually interested specifically in people's information needs, or needs that relate to the library's mission or purpose.

COMMUNITY NEEDS ASSESSMENT: an examination and analysis of the needs of all of the people a library serves.

USER NEEDS: the needs of the people who use the library.

LIBRARY NEEDS: things the library or library staff needs.

CUSTOMER SATISFACTION SURVEY: a series of questions asked of people who use the library that determines the degree to which they are pleased with the library, its programs, and services.

Many more books and articles in the library science literature address "user needs" or "library needs" than "community needs." Although some of the library science literature about needs assessment takes nonusers into consideration, overwhelmingly it focuses on library users' satisfaction with the library, and the library's needs. Of course, it is important for librarians to know how they are doing in the opinion of people who come into the library or who use the library's website; however, when it comes to planning effective library programs and services for the future, it is essential to understand the information needs of all of the people in the community, school, corporation, law office, university, or community college.

Some needs assessment literature in the library science field addresses evaluating what the library needs. When asked about needs, librarians commonly launch into a well-rehearsed list of what the library needs. Why does the library need these things? The answer lies in the incapacity of the library to do its work to meet the informational, educational, and/or recreational needs of people. Do not make the mistake of focusing on what the library needs without first finding out what people need.

ⓖ Planning an Effective Community Needs Assessment

Typically, identifying community needs happens in the initial stages of the strategic planning process. Knowing community needs helps determine the plan's objectives for meeting specific benchmarks. Reaching objectives helps to accomplish goals. If your library has a current strategic plan, you probably have conducted a community needs assessment recently. Otherwise, you would not have been able to make goals and objectives that relate to what people need. If your plan is three to five years old, you may want to update the needs assessment because communities and the people in them can change significantly over such a long period.

If your library has no strategic plan, or if you have filled in a generic template to substitute for a plan, many excellent resources are available on how to go through the planning process. For instance, Sandra Nelson's *The New Planning for Results: A Streamlined Approach* (2001) is a standard reference guide for strategic planning in public libraries. This book contains valuable information that can help librarians working in all library types go through the planning process—including the needs assessment phase.

There is no shortcut. You must find out what people need before you plan. Guessing doesn't count, nor does intuitively "knowing" what people need because you have been providing programs and services for the same community for decades. "We have always done it that way" is a much overused and tired phrase. Asking people who regularly attend programs and use library services if they are satisfied with the library is not a needs assessment; it is a customer satisfaction survey. Regular library users are by definition satisfied with the library. When you ask satisfied people if they are satisfied and you call it a needs assessment, you are manufacturing false data that make it look like you are meeting everyone's needs. You might even begin to believe this yourself.

It is tempting to keep this up by cultivating library users who give you positive feedback. It not only feels good to think you are doing so well, but it is much easier than considering the possibility that some people in your community have unmet information needs. Many of them may not even use the library because their needs have been ignored for so long. The longer you cater to a small circle of satisfied library customers, the more exclusive your library will become. By designing library services and activities for this select group, the library essentially separates itself from the larger community. As the years pass, generations of people do not use the library because they have learned that it is an exclusive place that has no real interest in meeting their needs. Don't let this happen in your library.

Use Your Community Profile

The community profile discussed in chapter 3 informs you about everyone you serve. It gives librarians a "big picture" of the people in their communities and emerging trends. Profiles tell public librarians about residents' demographics including people's ages, economic status, educational level, jobs or employment, language spoken at home, and migration trends, for instance. They tell librarians what schools, churches and synagogues, parks and recreational facilities, social services agencies, nonprofits, businesses, hospitals, and medical offices are in the community. If you are a school librarian, special librarian, or academic librarian, a community profile tells you about the people in your school or school district, academic institution, organization, or corporation. It provides details about people such as positions held, places of residence, academic achievement, test scores and grades, major accomplishments, and family income. A profile of the surrounding community will further enhance a special, academic, or school librarian's understanding of the people living in the geographic area where their library operates.

Supplement the community profile with other available information from the U.S. census, in public records and other research done on your community, reports about library use in general such as gender, age, educational level, income level, and numbers of children living at home. Compile, analyze, and synthesize all the information and data you have gathered. Use it to discover information needs or help you plan what questions to ask in the needs assessment.

Look to Your Organization and Others

Before you invest staff time and money in designing and conducting a community assessment, investigate other departments in your organization, corporation, municipality, academic institution, or school district for other recent community needs assessments. Even though an assessment by your larger organization may not have been designed specifically to assess information needs, you probably will be able to glean some important information from them that can inform your assessment design or help you decide important questions to ask. Inquire at local social services agencies, nearby schools or local educational institutions, and other nearby libraries about assessment data they are willing to share.

⑥ Understanding Community Needs Assessments

Effective community needs assessments involve assessing the entire community, not just the people who use the library or members of the friends' group. When businesses investigate their potential market to grow, they look at entire communities, regions, or online populations. They do not focus on the people who are already customers. If businesses focused on current customers, they would eventually shrink as the customer base got smaller and smaller. Soon they would go out of business. The same principle applies to libraries. Where libraries are concerned, the community consists of two segments: 1) the people who use the library and 2) the people who don't use the library. The portion of your community that uses the library differs from community to community; however, a recent study shows that 56 percent of people in the United States have used a public library in the past year (Zickuhr 2012).

Herbert Landau (2008) suggests a two-part approach to designing needs assessments. You can assess some obvious needs of current patrons by analyzing library cardholder data; analyzing circulation statistics; analyzing reference queries; conducting formal and informal surveys; interviews; and observation, for instance. Generally, librarians are very good at knowing the characteristics of their current patrons and their demographics, how many of them visit the library building and website, numbers of books they check out and e-books they download, numbers who attend programs, numbers and types of reference questions they ask, and how they use the library's website, for instance. They can tell you how satisfied their patrons are with the library building, furniture, parking, the collection, computers, the various programs offered, and overall performance of library staff. They may even be able to tell you what library users need and want. But library users are only a fraction of everyone you serve. Deciding what programs and services to offer based on the needs of library users alone can have long-range detrimental effects for your library and community.

Identifying the needs of library nonusers is more challenging. It involves not only defining the demographics of nonusers, but also identifying and prioritizing their education and information needs; locating and analyzing information about them in news media; attending community organization meetings and other places where they congregate; interacting with them in the community, school, college, or workplace; and conducting surveys, for example. Assessing nonusers' needs forces librarians outside the library and sometimes out of their comfort zone.

Case Study: Nonusers Are Community Members, Too

The Boonesville Community Library prides itself on offering quality children's programs and services. Although this public library is supposed to serve the entire community of Boonesville, it offers no programs for teens or adults. Librarians use all available resources for children's programming because they are so popular and attendance is high. Adults arrive and leave very quickly because no quiet place is set aside for them to read or congregate. Teens do not spend much time in the library with so many small children running around inside on most days. This significant segment of Boonesville's population has stopped going to the library because their needs are not only unmet—they are being ignored.

The library director conducted a community needs assessment in anticipation of strategic planning. Library staff distributed surveys to people who came into the library. Mostly parents, grandparents, day-care providers, and other child caregivers who accompanied children to the programs completed surveys. The survey asked questions such as the following: "Are you satisfied with the children's programs?," "Do you want more children's programs?," and "Is it easy to park when you attend children's programs?"

Survey results showed an overwhelming satisfaction and need for more children's programs and services. The survey showed very little need for teen and adult programs and services. So, the library director saw to it that the strategic plan included offering even more children's programs and services for the next five years. Teens and adults needs continued to be ignored, and they continued to stay away from the library.

What is wrong here? Don't the teens and adults in Boonesville have any information needs? How can children have the biggest needs when the library is already spending most of its resources on children?

Answer: Of course teens and adults in the community had unmet needs. Here are a few major problems with this community needs assessment:

1. The library director didn't have a broad view of the community and its needs to start. She was focused on the library and library users, specifically children and children's programs.
2. The survey didn't seek input from the entire community, specifically teens and adults who didn't use the library.
3. The survey asked the wrong questions.

Most teens and adults didn't have input. Determining community needs by surveying regular satisfied library users is irrational. Assessing users' needs or library needs and calling it a community needs assessment is wrong. It promotes ignoring what the community needs.

⊚ Finding Out What People Need

Decide what you want to know. Think about what people need in terms of your library's mission. Libraries usually fulfill an informational, educational, and/or recreational role in their communities, schools, colleges and universities, corporations, hospitals, law firms, and prisons. It is essential to keep the library's role in mind as you ask people what they need. Focus on what you can do within the parameters of your library's purpose. Which needs are most obvious and need attention more quickly than others? Which needs most greatly impact people's quality of life? Which unmet needs are taking excessive staff time? Which needs are you able to do something about? Are any ones you have overlooked in the past?

Consider narrowing the scope of the assessment to one or a few information-needs topics or specific aspects of current library programs and services. You can determine the topics from your community profile. This will make conducting a needs assessment more realistic. By conducting several smaller assessments, you can test the waters. This will help you to know how much time and effort an assessment will take, and you can try out some different methodologies on a smaller scale.

SUCCESSFUL ASSESSMENTS START WITH PLANNING

Librarians at the Via Christi Regional Medical Center Libraries (Kansas) conducted a thorough needs assessment designed to find out:

1. How the libraries could best serve their patrons and
2. How the libraries could best help the medical center improve patient care and outcomes.

First, librarians defined their potential customer base and geographic service area. Next, they collected data using three different instruments: telephone interviews, focus groups, and surveys. They involved as many existing and potential library users as possible. Users and nonusers responded to different question sets. They made surveys available in both print and electronic formats. This carefully designed and conducted needs assessment produced results that provided the necessary evidence to develop a user-centered strategic plan (Perley 2007).

Ask for input about needs that your library can address. Do not waste people's time by asking irrelevant questions or questions you can't do anything about. Participants will pick up on this right away, and they probably will ignore your efforts. Start with immediate and obvious needs that probably require attention sooner than later.

From your community profile, along with observation and data you have collected from other sources, you can likely identify some of the most important unmet needs. For instance, from experience you know that often people wait in line in your library to use the Internet computers, the computer sign-up sheets are always full, and patrons often complain about insufficient Internet computers in the library. By observing the situation, looking at the sign-up sheets, compiling computer usage statistics, and documenting complaints you probably can safely predict that people have unmet needs to access the Internet computers in your library. To clarify and document this perceived need, you probably would include a series of questions in your community needs assessment asking about Internet computers in the library and how people use the computers to meet their needs. Skillfully crafted questions yield just the information you need to improve the service.

If you cannot afford staff time to plan and conduct a needs assessment, or no one on your staff feels comfortable overseeing this effort, consider hiring an outside consultant. Your state library agency will have a list of library consultants for you to consider. Ask colleagues for recommendations. Interview prospective consultants, making sure they know how to do what you are asking and that they are a good fit for your organization. Be clear about their work scope, time line, and deliverables.

◎ Methodologies for Assessing Needs

Assessing needs involves both qualitative and quantitative methods of data collection and analysis. The idea is to generate usable answers that you can analyze and use to determine or improve library services and programs. There is no single right way to conduct a community needs assessment. One needs assessment can include several different methods. Triangulation is the use of more than one instrument for data collection to ensure credibility (Perley 2007). Listed below are some common methodologies:

- Surveys
- Interviews
- Focus groups
- Active participation
- Observation

Knowing both your community and the questions you want answered will help you determine the appropriate assessment methodologies. Consider appropriate methodologies for both library users and nonusers, people who visit the library building and people who use the website alike. This could mean using different tools for different segments of the population, or asking different questions of each group.

CREATING A DATA COLLECTION PLAN WORKSHEET

Use a worksheet like this to plan your data collection efforts. List your questions and put a check mark indicating whether you will look for the data in secondary sources (websites, community assessments already completed by other entities, or print resources such as newspapers) or primary sources (assessments you conduct yourself such as surveys, interviews, focus groups, etc.). Then list the method you will use to find or collect the data.

QUESTION	SECONDARY	PRIMARY	SOURCE OR METHOD
What are the basic demographics of the community such as income, race, employment, and educational level?	X		U.S. Census Bureau American FactFinder QuickFacts Town Annual Reports
What are the needs of teens in the community?	X	X	Secondary: U.S. Census for educational achievement levels or high school graduation rates Primary: Informal interviews with students hanging out in the park

Special accommodations may be necessary to reach parts of your community. For instance, if you know that some people in your community do not speak English, when you conduct a needs assessment you must provide surveys, conduct interviews, and hold focus groups in their native language to assess their needs effectively. If you are aware of a large senior population living in assisted living facilities with limited transportation options, you may need to visit them in their location to assess their needs. If you serve prison inmates who are restricted from using writing implements or computers, you will need to find an alternative to a written or computerized survey to assess their needs.

⊚ Conducting Community Needs Assessments

Surveys

Think carefully about what you want to know and ask questions that will yield useful results. Below are some tips for designing survey questions:

- Each question should be concise and contain a single thought
- Avoid double negatives
- Ask close-ended questions
- Do not "load" questions
- Eliminate bias
- Provide bilingual surveys
- Make surveys readable and visually appealing
- Provide alternative delivery methods
- Design different surveys for users versus nonusers
- Offer assistance
- Provide confidentiality and return postage

Information gained from surveys is only as good as the questions you ask. Be specific, and make every question count. Design your own survey. Do not substitute library surveys from other communities, even if the communities are nearby and may be similar to yours.

Phrasing is as important as formatting. Figure out how to phrase your questions in a way that will reveal the information you seek. Pretest your survey on family and friends to uncover discrepancies or questions that are unclear.

Different sets of questions might be appropriate for different groups. For instance, the set of questions you ask library users will be different from the questions you ask nonusers. You might want to ask nonusers why they don't use the library; however, you would not ask people who use the library this question. A survey to determine the needs of distance education stakeholders might ask students one set of questions about how the library supports their distance education studies, faculty another set of questions about how the library supports the courses they teach, and administrators other questions about their attitudes concerning the role of the library in distance education (Jerabek 2002). There are many ways to conduct community surveys. Here are a few:

- Mail to random community members
- Hand out to people on the street and in the library

- Distribute surveys in electric, water, or gas bills
- Distribute surveys at community meetings
- Go into schools
- Insert surveys in local publications
- Put an electronic version (or link to one) on your library's website
- Make surveys available in social services agencies and local businesses

Interviews

Interviewing people in the community can be an excellent way to gather information about needs. This will get you out of the library and potentially in touch with people who don't use the library. Reach out to diverse community groups, organizations, and clubs. Be careful about interviewing people who are using the library. This could be a good way to get new ideas about what the library might do in the future, but it is not a good way to get a balanced assessment of community needs. Your time is valuable. Use it wisely to gather reliable needs information that you can use.

Telephone interviews can be a good way to assess people's needs; however, these days telephone interviewees will probably be limited to people with landlines. Be aware that you cannot cold call anyone who is listed on the Do Not Call List. Some people don't answer their telephone when the caller is unknown to them. Below are some tips about interviewing:

- Look beyond your library
- Have an open mind
- Don't make assumptions
- Listen

Focus Groups and Community Forums

Focus groups are a marketing research tool that can be adapted effectively for library community needs assessment purposes. They are structured discussions lasting one to two hours that usually involve ten to twelve individuals from the community who share common experiences or knowledge. A leader or moderator keeps the discussion on track by asking open-ended questions using a carefully prepared script. Focus groups are meant to draw people out by expressing their opinions and encouraging discussion without the restrictions that usually come with surveys or questionnaires, for instance. Conducting focus groups can be time-consuming, and leading them successfully requires some expertise. As with surveys, it is important to determine what you want to know beforehand and create questions that are designed to find out this information.

Community forums are usually larger groups. All interested individuals in the community are invited to attend an open public meeting about the future of the library. An agenda and process are devised in advance, and a facilitator leads the forum. With both formats, a recorder takes notes and documents comments, ideas, and feedback expressed by participants in these meetings. With permission from participants, make a recording that you can use as a reference following the meeting and for purposes of analysis.

Active Participation

Those who have a strong interest in the programs and services the library provides must be involved in the needs assessment process. Stakeholders can offer a pool of resources for planning and conducting the needs assessment. They may help increase support and participation in the needs assessment, and involving them leads to greater commitment in implementing any new programs or services indicated by the needs assessment results (Jerabek 2002).

Stakeholders' insight about community trends and issues can be invaluable. Visit these people in a location and at a time that is convenient for them. Interview community organization and business leaders, and welcome opportunities to partner with others who have similar missions or goals. When you are out in the community talking about the library's mission, vision, and plans, it is likely that you will encounter others who might want to collaborate on working to meet similar community needs. You can target areas where they may not be meeting specific information needs where you have an interest.

Observation

Walk around your community, go to neighborhood events, attend community activities and meetings. Talk to people informally about the library, how they use the library, or what they would like to see in the library. Do they have unmet needs, or do they frequent a neighboring library because yours doesn't usually have what they need? Set up a booth at a local farmer's market or artists' event. Invite people to share their ideas and input about the library, and market the library at the same time. Make this easy for people. Don't ask for names or require them to fill out forms. Make notes and record your observations as you interact with people.

Observe how things work for people in the library. Put yourself in their shoes. Sign up for a computer and find out how long it takes. Watch people sitting down at a public computer. Is it easy for new users to figure out what to click on to do what they want? Do computers lock up or crash frequently? Is assistance readily available and nearby? How does this affect library users?

⊚ Compiling Data

Compiling qualitative results is much more straightforward than compiling quantitative results. For example, for surveys and interviews with close-ended questions, calculate the number of distinct responses in each population group. Keep separate totals for each group, such as students, faculty, and staff. Enter the numbers into a spreadsheet and create a visual such as a graph or chart to better illustrate results.

Qualitative results such as responses in focus groups and community forums, open-ended comments on a survey, or observations must be transcribed or recorded separately. Compiling and analyzing qualitative information is more time-consuming and not so easy to graph or chart. Depending on the complexity of the population you are assessing and/or the data sets you are compiling, you may want to create data collection worksheets to keep the data organized and easier to analyze.

Think ahead. Take advantage of this opportunity to ask all related questions that will give you information you can use to enhance or grow library services and programs into the near future. For instance, if you are assessing people's Internet computer needs, don't limit your questions to hardware. Ask related questions that might help you decide what software to purchase, what computer training sessions to offer or electronic resources to purchase. Think through everything you want to know that will help you meet library Internet computer needs. Cluster these similar questions in the needs assessment, or make this into a self-contained assessment. If you think your library might seek additional funding for Internet computers in the future, assess all relevant needs so you can document wide-ranging library computer needs for grant proposal components.

Needs assessment is not a one-time event. It must be conducted on a regular basis because communities are constantly changing. For instance, new immigrants readily relocate, and it is not uncommon for librarians to find themselves abruptly in the midst of a new community of immigrants whose needs they do not know (Cuban 2007). It is vital to be keenly aware of what information the people in this new community need so the library can help bridge the culture gap.

Although it is important to stay current with changing communities and emerging needs, it is not necessary to conduct comprehensive needs assessments frequently. By building the task of maintaining data and staying current about people and the community into their jobs, librarians can be aware of changing needs at any given time. Smaller-scale assessments can be conducted on an as-needed basis to help stay current.

Meaningful library community needs assessment examples that librarians can peruse as a way to prepare for designing their own assessments are few and far between. Some are listed below.

Beware of referring to user needs assessments, customer satisfaction surveys, library building needs assessments, librarian or staff needs assessments, or library technology needs assessments. Assessing the things in the library, what librarians need, or what the library needs is not productive. Look for examples that focus on the needs of people in the community. Once you have information about what people need, it will be easy to determine what the library needs.

- Needs Assessment for the Richmond (California) Public Library: Community Analysis and Analysis of Community Characteristics (http://www.rplf.org/down load/Richmond_Needs_Doc_090216_sm.pdf)
- Community Library Needs Assessment Components: Logan Heights Branch Library, San Diego Public Library (http://www.sandiego.gov/public-library/pdf/ logan_needs.pdf)
- Assessment in the MIT Libraries (http://libguides.mit.edu/mitlibrarysurveys)

⊚ Key Points

Once you know people's information needs, you can plan relevant library programs and services that are designed to serve the entire community. One proven way to find out about people's information needs is to conduct a community needs assessment. It is important to understand what a community needs assessment is—and what it isn't. Needs assessments take time and effort, so take the time to plan them correctly.

- Communities consist of library users and nonusers.
- Focus on what you can do within the parameters of your library's purpose.
- The survival of libraries depends on meeting people's needs.
- Do not make the mistake of focusing on what the library needs without first finding out what people need.
- What people need and what they want are different.
- Information gained from surveys is only as good as the questions you ask.
- Ask for input about needs that your library can address.
- Assessing needs involves both qualitative and quantitative methods of data collection and analysis.
- Needs assessment is not a one-time event.

Chapter 5 guides you through the process of dealing with the data you collect in the community needs assessment. Once you have organized the information, you can use it to make informed decisions about which programs and services to offer.

⊚ ▲ References

Cuban, Sondra. 2007. *Serving New Immigrant Communities in the Library.* Westport, CT: Libraries Unlimited.

Jerabek, Judy Ann. 2002. "The Answer You Get Depends on Who (and What) You Ask: Involving Stakeholders in Needs Assessments." *Journal of Library Administration* 37, no. 3/4: 387–95.

Landau, Herbert B. 2008. *The Small Public Library Survival Guide: Thriving on Less.* Chicago: American Library Association.

McClure, Charles R., and Paul T. Jaeger. 2009. *Public Libraries and Internet Service Roles: Measuring and Maximizing Internet Services.* Chicago: American Library Association.

Nelson, Sandra S. 2001. *The New Planning for Results: A Streamlined Approach.* Chicago: American Library Association.

Perley, Kathy M. 2007. "Conducting a User-Centered Information Needs Assessment." *Journal of the Medical Library Association* 95, no. 2 (April): 173–81.

Zickuhr, Kathryn. 2012. *Libraries, Patrons and E-books.* Washington, DC: Pew Research Center's Internet and American Life Project. http://libraries.pewinternet.org/files/legacy-pdf/PIP_Libraries_and_Ebook_Patrons%206.22.12.pdf.

Organizing, Analyzing, and Interpreting Assessment Results

THE IMMEDIATE RESULTS OF YOUR COMMUNITY NEEDS assessment will be in the form of raw data. You will have before you unorganized numbers from surveys and questionnaires; text collected from open-ended survey questions and interviews; notes from observations; and recordings of community meetings or focus groups, for example. Unorganized raw data itself is not useful for making decisions about which library programs and services to offer. When you organize, analyze, and synthesize the data into an understandable format, it becomes information you can use. Next, you must process and analyze the data and put it into a context that you and others can understand and use to make decisions and plan for the future.

Organizing the Data

Before you can analyze and interpret assessment results, you need to organize the data. You will develop your own work style throughout the assessment process, including organizational methods; however, whatever the method, you need to stay organized and keep track of all results from beginning to end. Your methods will depend on the instruments you used to collect the data, the format of the data, the questions you want answered, and the software you use (if any).

If you collected paper surveys, you will need to gather them together manually and organize them in a way to generate results that are useful for you. For instance, if you conducted a survey to determine how college students access information online, you may want to separate the surveys by students' academic majors if you want to find out the differences in accessing information from discipline to discipline. Suppose you asked community members if they needed instruction on how to use e-mail. If you want to know the degree to which senior citizens need instruction on how to use e-mail, you would first separate out the surveys submitted by seniors.

If you are using a spreadsheet program such as Excel or a database such as Access, you might begin by assigning each survey a unique identifier and entering all the responses from all the surveys in sequential order. Then you can sort or arrange the data in ways that are useful for you. If you conducted an online survey using a Web-based survey tool such as SurveyMonkey or Zoomerang, the data are usually collected and organized for you online where you can sort data and generate reports to meet your needs.

You may have responses to open-ended questions from a survey, text from a transcript, recordings from focus groups or interviews, or notes from observation sessions. Read the transcripts, notes, or narratives and listen to the recordings. Write down your impressions and note any significant points. Try organizing this data by question or topic so you can look across all responses for the same question or comments on the same topic and compare or contrast answers for similarities or differences.

As you organize the data, you will probably discover some unexpected results. Stay open to new ideas and new ways of organizing the data to determine needs for different groups, topics, and questions. Be willing to change or adapt your organizational methods midstream. The results will show you the best way to organize the data to get the answers to your questions. The whole point of assessing needs is to discover unmet needs, so surprises are a good thing. Stay flexible. You will have to organize and reorganize the data in different and creative ways to get the most out of the assessment and ultimately deliver effective programs and services.

Analyzing the Data

In practice, before conducting the assessment you should develop a plan for analyzing your data. The ideal time to plan strategies for analyzing the data is when you are identifying the questions to ask and determining how you will collect the data. This way you can anticipate if the data you collect using a particular tool or instrument will be in a format that can be analyzed effectively to answer your questions. When you think through the entire process in advance from beginning to end, often you are able to catch potential errors or misjudgments that could otherwise keep you from extracting the information you need. Prevent pitfalls by planning ahead.

Analyzing community needs data involves examining it in ways that reveal trends and relationships, ultimately answering questions about planning library services and programs that are grounded in what people need. Because you probably used several assessment tools and methodologies for your needs assessment, you likely collected both quantitative data and qualitative data. Analyzing the data takes different forms depending on whether it is qualitative or quantitative. It is important to match your analysis strategy to the kind of data you have and the types of questions you want to answer.

Statistical analysis is a discipline that requires education, knowledge, and expertise. If you have an "uneasy relationship" with numbers, you may want to seek advice from someone who is knowledgeable about working with statistics or spend some time acquiring the necessary skills (Van Epps 2012). You probably will want to hire a professional evaluator, statistician, or consultant for analyzing community needs data for larger cities, counties, states, and extensive regions with diverse populations. Librarians with basic statistics skills in smaller towns or villages, schools, organizations, agencies, or firms probably can analyze their own data. Librarians in large cities, school districts, or corporations may have access to a statistician who works on multiple projects for that entity. Academic librarians may be able to find help in their university's research office, grants office, or business and economic research center. Librarians in large organizations of all types may find that evaluators are on staff or available on a part-time, on-call, or temporary basis for analyzing organizational data.

Analyzing Quantitative Data

You can analyze quantitative data mathematically in many ways depending on the questions you want to answer. Librarians are very good at keeping and analyzing statistics, and they are familiar with using software to generate different reports that answer various kinds of questions. So, analyzing quantitative needs assessment data is not a stretch for most librarians. Tabulate the quantitative data to get a comprehensive view of what your data look like and to help you identify patterns. Computer programs such as Excel or Access are readily available and relatively easy to use. These programs come packaged with different versions of Microsoft Office, so if you have an Office suite in the library you may already have them. Because these programs are so common, possibly you can recruit library staff, board members, or volunteers with a working knowledge of this software to assist by entering data. Advanced data analysis software such as SPSS, SAS, or ATLAS-TI is probably not necessary unless you are hiring an evaluator who requires a specific software program to analyze results.

Quantitative data analysis results in descriptive statistics, including methods that help to see the data in a meaningful way, such as numerical counts, percentages, measures of tendency (e.g., mean, median, mode), and measures of variability (e.g., range, standard deviation, variance). Descriptive statistics can help you summarize data, find patterns, and identify key findings. Figure 5.1 illustrates a simple table and graph displaying descriptive statistics.

Analyzing Qualitative Data

Qualitative data analysis is an ongoing, fluid, and cyclical process. It is dependent on the nature of the assessment and the kinds of questions you asked. The idea here is to discover patterns and themes that can help determine needed library programs and services. Focus groups, interviews, or community forums yield qualitative data such as descriptions, anecdotes, opinions, quotes, and interpretations in the form of text, transcripts, or recordings. The value of these data lies in its narrative nature, and it cannot be reduced to numbers without losing its inherent value. How you compile and use these results is likely to change as the data analysis process progresses. You must be open

Age Group	% of Population	% of Responses
8-12	4%	4%
12-15	6%	4%
16-18	6%	3%
19-21	10%	8%
22-26	15%	6%
27-35	13%	10%
36-45	14%	16%
46-55	12%	21%
56-65	9%	15%
Over 65	11%	13%

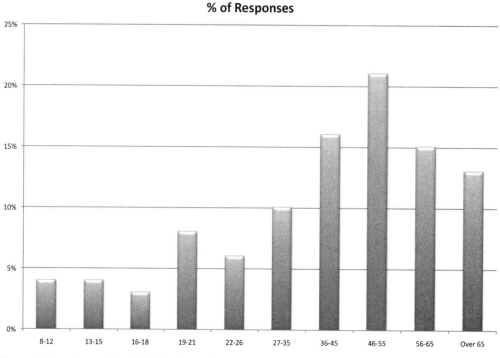

Figure 5.1. Descriptive Statistics Examples.

to discovering new and unexpected patterns and willing to explore new connections if you want to get the most out of qualitative data analysis. This can be anti-intuitive because when most people think of data analysis, they usually think of a dry and exact science. In fact, although analyzing qualitative data requires discipline and a systematic approach, it is also a creative process.

Focus on what you want to find out. Most qualitative data are not 100 percent relevant to the questions you want answered. Make choices about which aspects of the data you should emphasize and which you should minimize or eliminate. Knowing the questions you want answered will help you determine if a comment is relevant for this assessment. This is not to say that some comments are not at all important; it only means that for the purposes of this particular assessment, some comments are not pertinent. To make qualitative analysis more streamlined and focused, leave out irrelevant comments for now. You can always go back at a later date and use these comments to design a new assessment or explore new directions.

Use identifiers to designate the respondent, age group, meeting site, place of residence, or other source. Depending on the question at hand, you may want to sort data by variables such as age, site, or neighborhood. Use the demographic variables that relate to the questions you want answered. The identifiers will help you sort the data. If you are working with paper copies, a color-coding method may work best for you. Again, librarians are naturals at categorizing and classifying information, so this part should not be difficult.

Read and reread the text or listen and relisten to the recordings. You may need to transcribe recordings or write a summary of what people said. Look for key ideas, concepts, beliefs, or behaviors. Identify common themes and organize them into categories; then assign an abbreviation, symbol, or color to each category. Be clear about what you include in each category. Write a description for each category, especially if more than one person will be doing this activity. Place the code, abbreviation, symbol, or color next to the themes or ideas in the transcripts, meeting notes, or texts. Figure 5.2 illustrates some possible categories and abbreviations from a small sample of open-ended questions asked on a survey given to corporate employees.

Question	Responses
What is the most important service or program the library is or should be offering?	The library needs to be a source of state of the art research (RES). The library is a place (SP) where employees can get assistance from library staff (ST) locating and accessing information for marketing research (RES). The library should be a quiet place (SP) where employees can go to read professional journals and current literature (MAT). The library provides a place where colleagues can meet, share ideas and work on projects (MS). The library is a web-based (WE) hub for current electronic information (EL) in my field. The library should have apps for accessing all electronic library materials (EL) from anywhere.
Categories	

RES = Research
ST = Staff: Includes all library employees
SP = Library's physical space
    MS = Meeting spaces
MAT = Library Materials: Print and non-print items
    EL = Electronic information
WE = Web, website or web-related programs/services

Figure 5.2. Identifying Categories.

As you categorize you may find other relevant themes or subthemes. Stay open-minded. Continue to categorize and subcategorize until you have covered all aspects of the topics you want to cover and questions you want answered. Your list of categories may change as you work. You may need to create new categories or adjust definitions. Don't stress. This is the nature of qualitative analysis. In the end you will need as many categories as are necessary to reflect and interpret the data fully within the context of the questions you want answered.

Once you have labeled the data with categories, "cut and sort" the data, combining all the data labeled with one theme. If you are working in a word processing program, cut and paste text into a new document for each category. If you are working with hard copy, physically cut out the text with scissors and place it in piles or tape it onto papers that correspond to each category. If one passage pertains to multiple categories, copy the passage multiple times and place one copy in each category. Keep the source of the data with all of the data.

Data Analysis Tips

- Acquire basic statistical analysis skills.
- Keep it simple.
- Review and clean the data.
- Assign a unique identifier to each responder.
- Identify themes or patterns and organize them into categories.
- Assign an abbreviation or symbol to each category.
- Define each category.
- Use controlled vocabularies.
- Configure fields to reduce the possibility of data entry errors.
- Allow enough time and money for analysis.

⑥ Interpreting the Results

Analysis will help you describe and summarize results, identify key findings, notice patterns, and observe emerging themes; however, you still need to interpret the results and draw conclusions. If you made an effort to notice patterns and themes while you organized and analyzed the data, you probably have already come to some informal conclusions. Data alone, the information from analyzing the data, your hunches, or a list of findings will not tell you what you need to know. You must put these pieces together and come to formalized conclusions. Synthesizing the information you gleaned from the analysis and attaching meaning to it will enable you to make some decisions about what are essential library services and programs for your community.

Determining Patterns

Once you have sorted and analyzed the data, think about how the categories fit together and relate. Determine the importance of patterns and connections by counting the number of times a particular theme occurs or the number of respondents who mention certain themes. Counts can provide a rough estimate and illustrate a general pattern of relative importance. This is not a statistically sound method; however, it can be sufficient to give you some direction in determining the importance of certain issues from the community's perspective. Ask yourself these questions:

1. What patterns or common themes are emerging?
2. What do they say about what library services and programs are needed?
3. Are there deviations from the patterns? What are they? Can you explain them?
4. What do the results show about unmet information needs?

Next, map connections and relationships between and among categories. How do the categories fit together and relate? To track connections you can use note cards or sticky notes, draw diagrams, or create a matrix. If you feel creative, use colored markers and draw different shapes to represent different concepts. Document your reasons for making the connections so you can explain them to others and help them follow your thinking. Put your interpretations into the context of your library's vision and mission, and the community.

Consider What "Should Be"

Needs are the gap between what "currently is" and what "should be in the future." How do you know what "should be?" Your assessment results will reveal something about this gap for your community, and the library's mission and vision will guide you in using this information to close the gap. At the same time, when you are thinking about this gap it is important to be forward-thinking and to make yourself aware of where libraries are headed in the future. To position your library for growth opportunities, you need to embrace a "discovery-oriented outlook" (Mathews 2012, 5). Brian Mathews suggests that librarians too often look through microscopes when it comes to assessment, focusing on improving current services and programs rather than looking through telescopes to foresee new opportunities.

Investigate what is happening in other libraries, read current professional publications, and research national and state studies about trends, new innovations, and standards. Keep yourself informed about the future of libraries and don't get stuck in old paradigms. Think about the future in a realistic, yet forward-thinking context. This may help you envision library services and programs you never dreamed of and realize you can stop doing certain things because they are not meeting needs. Assessment is not all about finding out which new programs or services to add or adapt; it is also about knowing which ones to eliminate. You don't want to spend time, money, and energy on programs and services that are not meeting needs. Instead, maximize your value by replacing useless activities with services and programs that people really need.

Investigate relevant information from other sources to help you draw conclusions. Demographic statistics are plentiful. Certain population segments have consistent needs and preferences regardless of where they are located, their ethnic makeup, race, religion, or economic status. This is not always true in every community; however, it can be helpful to use this kind information if you think it may support or substantiate your results. For example, one report states that people sixty-five and over account for about 30 percent of visually impaired individuals; 19 percent of people seventy and older have visual impairments; and older Americans can expect to live longer than ever before (Desai et al. 2001). If your community is a retirement community, you can cite this report to support your assessment results indicating that most community members need a visually accessible website.

Numerous reports about library services and programs, trends, and performance measures are available. Begin at your state library agency for data about other libraries like yours in your state. The Institute of Museum and Library Services (IMLS), the American Library Association (ALA), Special Libraries Association (SLA), Public Libraries Association (PLA), American Association of School Librarians (AASL), and Association of

College and Research Libraries (ACRL) are a few resources where you can find current data about similar libraries. For example: A recent IMLS report states that U.S. town libraries have an average of 4.3 Internet computers per five thousand people (Swan et al. 2013). Your town library has four Internet computers for ten thousand residents, and your community responded that they need more access to Internet computers in the library. Use the information in the IMLS report about what "should be" in libraries like yours to substantiate your conclusions that an estimated additional five computers may be required in your library to meet people's information needs.

The Pew Research Center asked Americans ages sixteen through twenty-nine about possible new library services. They were most interested in:

- Apps that would let them locate materials in the library
- Apps for accessing library services on their phone
- Library kiosks throughout the community that would make library materials available (Zickuhr, Rainie, and Purcell 2013)

So, if responses from teens and young adults in your community indicated a need for more useful library apps to access library services, or if they had some innovative ideas about delivering information, refer to the Pew study for supplemental information about what "should be."

Regarding academic library trends, *Library Journal*'s 2010 Mobile Libraries Survey showed that 44 percent of academic library respondents offered "some type of mobile services." In its annual survey, Ball State University found that 73 percent of students reported using a smartphone in 2012 as compared with 27 percent in 2009. About 30 percent of the university's students reported owning a tablet (Duis 2013) and 67 percent of college students use their smartphones to search for specific information "often" (Laird 2012).

Reporting

Now take time to think about what you will be doing with the assessment results. It has been some time since you decided to conduct a needs assessment, and it is important to make sure you are still on track about its purpose. It is easy to become consumed with the assessment and data analysis activities and forget for a moment why you are doing this.

Chances are that at some point you will be presenting the results to others as you make a case for which library programs and services to offer in the future. Possibly the strategic planning committee will read the assessment report as they work on the library's three-year plan. Maybe library staff and members of the library board will read the report as they consider new initiatives for the coming year. Even if you are the only staff member in your library and you don't anticipate any inquiries about why you are providing certain programs and services, it is still good practice to prepare a report of your findings and conclusions. Writing a report will prepare you to explain why you are doing what you are doing to others such as your constituents, your supervisor, or potential partners.

The report is a summary of the information from your assessment in descriptive terms, including your conclusions. Keep your audience in mind. Develop a list of key points or important findings you discovered as a result of analyzing the data. Using this list, create an outline for presenting your results in a report. Keep your report concise and to the point. Use anecdotes or stories that illustrate a need. Quotes are usually compelling. Visual displays such as charts, graphs, and tables can communicate numerical and statistical information in a digestible format. To conclude, answer the following questions:

- What did you learn?
- What does it mean?
- What community needs are most important?

Before you finalize the report, involve stakeholders. Review your findings and conclusions with them, and seek their input. Ask them if your reasoning seems logical, if anything looks questionable, or if any points need clarification. It is always wise to seek an objective opinion from someone who was not involved in conducting the needs assessment. Find out from stakeholders if other organizations or agencies are working to meet any of the most important needs. For instance, if literacy rises to the top of most important community needs, it is important to know if a program, group, or organization in your community is already working on improving literacy.

If you think you might seek a grant or other alternative funding to pay for future library services or programs, a needs assessment and final report will provide the information you need to justify the needs in your proposal. Conducting a needs assessment is not part of proposal writing. You must be prepared in advance with data, information, and needs assessment results well before you begin to look for funding to meet needs.

⑥ Prioritizing the Needs

Prioritizing needs is a great opportunity to involve others. You have done the hard work to plan and conduct the assessment, organize and analyze the results, come to some conclusions, and prepare a report. Now is a good time to share your assessment results with other staff, members of the community, and stakeholders. You already know the assessment results and the most-important needs; however, how do you decide what to address first? It is important to welcome others' opinions and viewpoints for several reasons. First, it is possible that you could have missed an important point or failed to include some essential information that would influence your findings. Next, extending yourself to staff, stakeholders, and the community at large to present the results and seek their input prior to making "final" decisions about priorities is always good practice. You will get their buy-in, and you might find partners, collaborators, and allies to help implement future programs and services. By involving a well-balanced cross section of people in the process, you will take the wind out of the sails of potential critics. If you are assessing and prioritizing as part of the strategic planning process, the planning committee must be involved. For public libraries, board participation is essential. Invite supervisors, CEOs, principals, mayors, business leaders, officers from local clubs, and town council members.

Present your report and findings, including what you have determined to be the most important needs. Explain your logic or reasons for concluding which needs are most important. Cover the data you used to come to your conclusions. Show visuals in the form of graphs, diagrams, matrixes, and models. Keep it simple. Figure 5.3 shows a simple table that contains information about how various age groups ranked library services and programs by importance. Color-coding like items in this chart makes it easy to visualize priorities.

AGE GROUP	#1	#2	#3	#4	#5
10-12	Homework Programs	Children's Reading Programs	Arts Programs	Public Computer Access	Library Website
13-16	Homework Programs	Craft Programs for Teens	Teen Gaming Night	Public Computer Access	Library Website
17-21	Online Databases	Quiet Study Areas	English Language Skills Programs	Teen Gaming Night	Craft Programs for Teens
22-26	Library Website	Children's Story Hour	Career Center	Online E-Books Collection	English Language Skills Programs
27-34	Homework Programs	Library Website	Children's Reading Programs	English Language Skills Programs	Basic Literacy Programs
35-44	Homework Programs	Craft Programs for Teens	Career Center	Teen Gaming Night	Community Meeting Rooms
45-54	Career Center	Computer Training	Adult Reading Areas	Best Selling Books	English Language Skills Programs
55-64	Wireless Internet Access	Adult Reading Areas	Art Exhibits	Reference Service	Best Selling Books
65 and over	Computer Training	Public Access Computers	Reference Service	Adult Reading Areas	Art Exhibits

Figure 5.3. Most Important Library Programs/Services Ranked by Age Group.

List four or five of the highest priorities and identify other agencies or organizations already addressing aspects of these needs. Brainstorm ideas for collaborating with others to implement new library services and programs, supplement what is being offered by others, or improve current library offerings. Although this is a time for sharing and getting input from others, the assessment report remains the same. Welcome different opinions and be open to incorporating new ideas; however, don't alter the assessment report. Ideally it is an accurate summary of the data you collected and it is not open to interpretation.

Determining the Needs Your Library Should Address

One important question to ask before you decide which needs your library will address is: How well suited is the library to meeting the need? (Nelson 2001). Just because an information need is unmet does not mean that it is appropriate for the library to address. After you decide which needs are most important, you may find that another agency is already meeting a need, or a need is not in line with the library's mission. For instance, although the library may offer some "recreational" programs, building a community swimming pool to meet a need is not within the scope of the library's work.

If a prioritized need falls within the mission of the library and is not being met elsewhere in the community, is it realistic for the library to undertake? Never reject the opportunity to meet a need with a new program or service just because the library doesn't have enough money, staff, space, resources, or anything else. This kind of deficit thinking will prevent you from growing innovative library programs and services into the future. It could keep you from meeting needs at all, and eventually your users will disappear along with your funding. Using the fact that you have always done things a certain way and it has always worked is not a good reason to resist change. The purpose of this exercise is to identify problems and find solutions. Solving problems is not usually easy, and it often means doing things differently than you have always done them.

Some librarians want to conduct library needs assessments at the same time they are doing community needs assessments. The challenge with assessing what the library needs before you know people's information needs is that you cannot base the library's needs on people's needs. You must know what community needs you plan to meet before you can determine if the library has the capacity to meet them. Focusing on what the library needs because the library doesn't have it is circular thinking. Dig deeper. Why does the library need these things? How will they benefit people?

The time to assess the library is after you know which programs and services you will provide and you have designed a plan, including a budget. Then a library assessment will tell you if the library has what is needed to implement the new programs and services. Here's the good news: If the library's capacity falls short, then you will know what the library must have to meet people's information needs. You are effectively equipped to seek alternative funding or financial help from the friends' group or community service groups, for instance, when you know exactly what you need to benefit people in specific ways. You will find that attracting funding is much easier when you can articulate where the money will be spent to help provide specific programs and services versus saying the library is poor and needs money. Funders want to give money for a specific purpose. They want to know how people will benefit.

⊚ Key Points

After you conduct the needs assessment, you must organize, analyze, and interpret the data. The methods you choose to do this will depend on the tools and instruments you used to conduct the assessment and the questions you want answered. Prepare a report of assessment results to share with stakeholders and for use by others in planning.

- Before you can analyze and interpret assessment results, you need to organize the data.
- Before you conduct the assessment, develop a plan for analyzing your data.
- Match your analysis strategy to the kind of data you have and the questions you want answered.
- Focus on what you want to find out.
- Expect the unexpected.

- Stay open-minded and look for new opportunities.
- Look for patterns and relationships.
- Involve stakeholders.
- Investigate relevant information from other sources to help you draw conclusions.
- A report summarizes the information from your assessment in descriptive terms.
- Assessment is also about knowing which programs and services to eliminate.
- Prioritizing needs is a great opportunity to involve others.
- Ask how well suited your library is to meet a need.
- Never reject an idea for meeting needs because the library doesn't have enough money, staff, space, resources, or anything else.

The next chapters will cover the process of designing a service, program, or project. Project design includes identifying the resources you will need to implement it, including personnel, equipment, supplies, space, and funding. In chapter 6 you will begin to design innovative ways to meet the needs of your specific community. The chapter explains the seven core elements of every successful library program or service.

References

Desai, Mayur, Laura A. Pratt, Harold Lentzner, et al. 2001. *Trends in Vision and Hearing Among Older Americans.* Hyattsville, MD: National Center for Health Statistics.

Duis, Sarah. 2013. "College Students Replacing Laptops and Desktops with Smartphones and Tablets." *USA Today College*, May 20. http://www.usatodayeducate.com/staging/index.php/ccp/college-students-replacing-laptops-and-desktops-with-smartphones-and-tablets.

Laird, Sam. 2012. "In a Relationship: College Students and Their Smartphones." *Mashable.* June 30. http://mashable.com/2012/06/30/smartphones-college-students-infographic/.

Mathews, Brian. 2012. "Too Much Assessment Not Enough Innovation." Paper presented at the *Library Assessment Conference.* Charlottesville, VA. http://vtechworks.lib.vt.edu/bitstream/handle/10919/19047/Too_Much_Assessment_R%26D_Paper_Mathews_Enhanced_Version.pdf?sequence=1.

Nelson, Sandra S. 2001. *The New Planning for Results: A Streamlined Approach.* Chicago: American Library Association.

Swan, Deanne W., Kim A. Miller, Terri Craig, et al. 2013. *Public Libraries Survey: Fiscal Year 2010.* Washington, DC: Institute of Museum and Library Services.

Van Epps, Amy S. 2012. "Librarians and Statistics: Thoughts on a Tentative Relationship." *Practical Academic Librarianship: The International Journal of the SLA Academic Division* 2, no. 1: i–xiii.

Zickuhr, Kathryn, Lee Rainie, and Kristen Purcell. 2013. *Younger Americans' Library Habits and Expectations.* Washington, DC: Pew Research Center's Internet & American Life Project. http://libraries.pewinternet.org/2013/06/25/younger-americans-library-services/.

Part II

PLANNING SERVICES AND PROGRAMS THAT MAKE A DIFFERENCE

CHAPTER 6

Designing Effective Programs and Services

IN THIS CHAPTER

▷ Planning is essential

▷ Understanding the characteristics of effective programs and services

▷ Incorporating the basic elements into the design

▷ Forming a team

NOW THAT YOU KNOW WHAT YOUR COMMUNITY NEEDS, how do you provide it? What format will the library's programs, services, or projects take? Which staff members and how many are required to make a program happen? How much will it cost? The answers are in the planning. Please keep reading. Planning is not necessarily the boring, dry, and long, drawn-out process you may have been led to believe. Planning can be the exciting part when you can create opportunities at the library that will make the most difference for people. This is when you can put your talents and strengths to work, collaborating with other staff members and stakeholders to build creative, innovative, and effective programs and services. Whether or not you know it, if you have conducted a needs assessment, analyzed the results, and prioritized needs, then you have already begun the planning process. The next step is to design or plan programs and services to meet the prioritized needs.

Planning Is Essential

In some libraries, designing effective programs and services is a part of strategic planning. In others, librarians lead teams or committees in planning programs and services following strategic planning. Your library's organizational functioning will lead the way. In a small public library with a small staff, all library employees might be involved in planning all programs and services with the director taking the lead. In a larger public library with department heads for adult services, children's services, and teen services, for instance, the department heads will likely lead the efforts for planning programs and services to meet the needs of their target populations. If your large academic or corporate library functions by committee, then committees will do the work of planning programs and services. Most librarians don't appoint large teams that include all levels of staff to plan every program and service. This would make the process unwieldy and difficult. Consider including community members to keep you focused on what is important.

Planning can be one of the most rewarding parts of library work. This is when you put pencil to paper and create programs and services that are unique to your community and library. You, library staff, and stakeholders decide what to do for the benefit of the community and figure out the best way to do it. You can create offerings that no other library has seen before or partner with other organizations to reach a goal.

Library work is more rewarding when program and service plans offer specific goals to accomplish. When you have stated objectives and ways to measure your success, you can celebrate how your program benefited people or improve on what you are doing. Plans tell you what you intend to accomplish, the steps to take to provide programs or services, the staff needed to implement them, the resources needed and how much they will cost, how long it will take, and how to measure success. A few more good reasons for strategic planning are listed below. Strategic planning:

- Helps you find real solutions
- Helps you see issues from multiple perspectives
- Translates visions and missions into specific goals and objectives
- Helps you make progress
- Helps you make a difference for people
- Informs you and others about what you are doing and why
- Helps you lead effectively
- Facilitates change and helps to overcome ineffective practices
- Creates connections between agencies, people, and organizations
- Helps you use resources wisely
- Enables you to acquire grants and alternative funding

Librarians and Planning

It is no secret that the mention of "strategic planning" prompts eye-rolling and audible sighs in a roomful of librarians. Why? Here are a few possibilities. Many librarians graduate from library school without having taken a course in strategic planning, or one that includes any comprehensive instruction on planning. Librarians with no training or experience in the strategic planning process don't know where to start. Admittedly, it is daunting to consider not only learning about strategic planning, but also taking on the responsibility of leading the planning effort in your library. But effective programs and services don't happen by accident. It is not an option to guess or continue to do what has always worked in the past. Communities are changing faster than ever, and technology continues to transform our field at a remarkable pace. Librarianship is not a stagnant field; librarians must change—and change briskly at times—if they want to stay in the game. Plans are a pathway to providing effective library programs and services amid constant change.

Library directors who are required by their state library agency, university, corporation, or school district to prepare strategic plans without being given the training or tools to plan are at a distinct disadvantage. Many seek the quickest way to get through this distasteful assignment. They want to do the least amount of work possible so they can get back to running the library. The easiest way to submit a strategic plan that meets the minimum criteria may be to fill in a template. A librarian can single-handedly fill in the blanks in a few hours with information about the library that has very little to do with meeting community needs and requires no actual planning. Plans like this are a disservice to libraries, library staff, and communities alike.

One reason some librarians resist change and insist on doing what they've always done may be because they aren't confident about deciding what else to do. Without a plan, making changes or providing new and innovative programs and services can be scary. When a team creates a plan to meet community needs, the plan will tell you what to do and give you the confidence to do it. Your decisions won't be guesses, and they won't be about your personal feelings. Plans minimize risk. Even if you start small by focusing on one or two prioritized needs, planning is necessary. You must start somewhere if you want results.

Librarians without education or training in strategic planning can learn on the job if they are fortunate enough to work in organizations that include library staff in organizational planning activities. You may be able to find a mentor in your organization who is willing to guide and coach you. Continuing education classes, university courses, and online workshops on strategic planning are available. Entire books on library planning have been written specifically for librarians. The resources are plentiful, rendering bad or nonexistent library plans inexcusable. Bad or nonexistent plans can cause:

- Miscommunication
- Lack of understanding about what you are doing and why
- Obstructed pathways to success
- Poor results
- Failed programs and services
- Unmet community needs
- Wasted money and resources
- Bigger divide between the library and nonusers
- Wasted time, effort, and money

Without planning you won't know what to do; you won't know why you are doing what you are doing; and you won't know if what you are doing is making a difference.

Librarians and Statistics

Historically, librarians have documented what they are doing and measured their success primarily by citing statistics. For instance, some believe that increased circulation statistics, more people visiting the library, rising numbers of web hits, increased program attendance, and the acquisition of more library materials, databases, and online products mean a library is successful. Causing numbers to increase doesn't require strategic planning; rather, a good marketing strategy to your best users and some statistical manipulation of your best features will do the trick. For librarians whose superiors are convinced by statistics, it has not been difficult to avoid strategic planning.

A problem lies with thinking your library is successful because you have stellar statistics to prove it. It makes no sense and it no longer works. Today, librarians must be accountable to their communities; they need to provide effective programs and services that make a difference for people; they must spend funds wisely on relevant materials, electronic resources, and products; and they must prove their worth. The fact that library visits increased 10 percent over the past year does not indicate success. This might have happened because the sidewalk in front of the library was under construction for eight months, during which time sidewalk traffic was detoured through the library. Conversely, if library visits decreased 10 percent over the past year, it doesn't mean the library is failing. It could be because more people are accessing the library on the Web, which recorded 25 percent more hits. Counting is no way to measure a library's success. Good planning is essential.

Understanding the Characteristics of Effective Programs and Services

Effective library programs and services have some common characteristics. They:

- Align with the library's mission
- Help meet real needs and make a real difference for people

Align with Library's Mission

Now that you've spent quality time determining community needs and prioritizing them, ensure that your prioritized needs align with the library's mission. It doesn't hurt to read the mission statement frequently. Post it on the wall where you can easily refer to it any time. This is good practice, even when you are not in the midst of planning. It is not uncommon for people to find as they go through this process that the prioritized needs are not exactly within the library's role. If you discover this, you may need to select one aspect of a need to address and partner with another agency to address another aspect. Or you might decide that the library's mission statement needs updating. If you haven't conducted a community needs assessment in a very long time, the community could have changed to the extent that the library's mission is no longer a good fit for the community. If you don't read the mission statement very often or constantly use it to help you determine what to do, you may temporarily lose track of your library's mission, role, or purpose. When a disconnect occurs, the library's purpose, what it is offering, and the community's needs exist on different planes without connecting or relating to each other. If you are in this situation, you have lost your way. Don't worry. The important thing is to be aware. Then you can do something about it. First be clear about the needs and the mission statement, making sure they are aligned.

Once your mission statement is current and accurate, you have recently assessed and prioritized the community's needs, and you are routinely designing programs and services with these things in mind, you will not need to check the mission statement so often. At some point you will begin to see that meeting needs, the library's mission, and program or service design are all interconnected. When things are working well, the synchronicity will assume a real meaning for you, and it will make a difference in the work you do and how you do it.

If you have ever worked in a library where no one knows (or can find) the library's mission statement or strategic plan, and community needs assessment has not been conducted, you know from experience how disorienting this can be. You cannot get your footing because you lack solid ground, a horizon to aim for, and a path to take. In cases like this, you cannot do your best work as a librarian, and your strengths and talents are often wasted. Ultimately the community loses. Don't let this happen in your library.

Take a few minutes to complete the following exercise. It will help you to see how your programs and services are aligned with your library's mission.

CURRENT PROGRAM AND SERVICE ALIGNMENT EXERCISE

List the programs and services your library offers and how each one aligns with the library's mission. Examples of services are reference, public computers, online catalog, interlibrary loan, web-based services, readers' advisory, and outreach services. Program examples include story hours, humanities programs, art exhibits, performances, homework help, information literacy programs, teen craft clubs, adult reading groups, computer classes, English language learning programs, literacy programs, and movie nights. Refer to your library's mission statement and list which part of the mission statement is fulfilled by the service or program.

CURRENT SERVICE	HOW IT ALIGNS WITH LIBRARY'S MISSION

CURRENT PROGRAM	HOW IT ALIGNS WITH LIBRARY'S MISSION

Help Meet Real Needs and Make a Difference for People

Effective library services and programs must meet real needs and make a real difference. Take a moment to focus on the needs that have top priority for your library and try to understand their underlying causes. Knowing why these needs exist will inform the project design and will make meeting them much easier. When you truly understand why a problem or need exists, you can increase your ability to help solve it—maximize the impact of what you do.

For instance, imagine that the needs assessment of students in your school showed poor English language proficiency. Why? Your school profile reveals that 20 percent of the students attending your school are non-English speakers. Where are they from, and what languages do they speak? Your community profile indicates an influx of immigrants into your community in recent years who speak Spanish, Hmong, and Somali. Now that you know more about the underlying causes for poor English language proficiency among students at your school, you can provide meaningful programs and other support for these students, possibly in their native languages. You might use this knowledge to design additional programs to help English language learners in your school—for example, bilingual homework assistance or writing programs. Or, you could put links on your school's website to community services for immigrants from other countries, or links to online language learning programs for parents available through the public library.

When you understand root causes, you also will have the insight to discover or attract partners and collaborators who have the capacity to work with you on your project or who can meet additional needs for the same population. Conversely, if other agencies are addressing similar issues, you can step forward to work with them by supplementing or enhancing what they are providing. Combining efforts offers more comprehensive and connected services. The potential for making a bigger difference and significantly changing people's lives increases dramatically when you work in concert with other agencies and organizations to address common issues and their underlying causes. Limited English proficiency among students does not happen in a vacuum. Entire immigrant families likely have numerous information and other needs.

When you stab at solutions to problems you don't understand very well, you will be more likely to fail or have limited success. You might even alienate people if you lack enough sensitivity to their problems. For instance, 75 percent of seniors in your community may not use the public library even though 85 percent of them need health information. Unless you know why, you might purchase health materials for seniors, hoping they will attract more of this population into the library. But what if seniors don't go to the library because it is always packed with noisy children and doesn't offer a place for adults to sit and read quietly? Maybe many seniors are physically unable to navigate the library's narrow and meandering passageways safely. You can get to the bottom of some issues by asking the right questions in your needs assessment.

Taking the time to sense where people are coming from or what it is like to face their problems will give you compassion for their situation. When you care about helping people, you are more likely to be interested in understanding underlying issues and partnering with others to address the big picture. Libraries and librarians are not separate from the community. You are part of your community. The community's problems are your problems, too. As you go through the planning process, try to see program and service design as something that will help you and everyone around you.

Beware of Popular Trends

We live in a world where smart businesses and corporations spend lots of time and money to promote their latest products, trying to get people—such as librarians—to buy into their advertising. Particularly since technology came to the forefront, librarians have had to be very careful about not succumbing to "techno-lust," or the urge to buy new technology for its own sake. This does not mean that librarians should avoid new technology or popular trends. It only means that librarians must be careful about adapting a new technology, product, tool, or innovation simply because it is a popular trend. By all means, use new technology when it can help you implement a program or service, if it will enhance what the library offers, if it will help you reach people or make a difference for people, or increase your chances of success. A gimmick for one library might be just what another library needs to help fulfill its mission or reach a goal. Only you can judge for your library. When you find yourself considering a new product or tool that is highly publicized and you notice librarians everywhere are suddenly implementing it, before you follow the crowd ask yourself how it will help meet your community's needs. Some trends that have captured librarians' attention in recent years include espresso book machines, 3-D printers, bookless libraries, video gaming, and makerspaces.

◎ Incorporating the Basic Elements into the Design

Every program, project, or service design needs these core elements:

- Goals
- Objectives
- Outcomes
- Activities
- Time line
- Budget
- Evaluation plan

When you create these elements step-by-step, you will have a program, project, or service design (see figure 6.1).

If you have not planned programs and services using these components in the past, try it. You will see how valuable this approach can be for the effectiveness and success of your library. Designing programs and services this way does not have to be a long, drawn-out process. In fact, for smaller programs it can be very straightforward. Once you are familiar with the process, you will be able to design simple projects fairly easily and you will find that it is well worth the effort. Employing this method will help you clarify what you are doing and why. It is a way to connect all programs and services to the library's mission and goals. It will give staff members a common understanding about what they are doing and why. It is a tool for determining the resources you will need, including staff, supplies, equipment, consulting fees, space, and materials or products. It helps you to see where you can use partners and what you need them to do. It will provide you with measurable objectives and a way to determine if programs and services are accomplishing your desired goals. This way of planning will give you tools you can use to

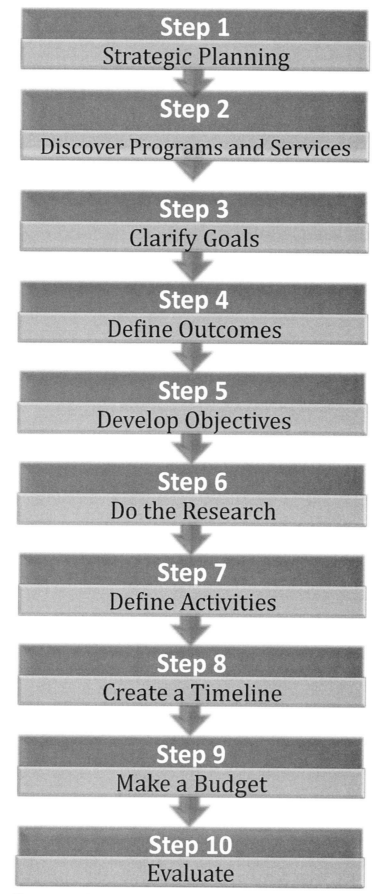

Figure 6.1. Steps To Design a Library Program or Service.

market or promote the library by showing how programs and services make a difference. Solid designs will lay the groundwork for seeking alternative funding by providing you with the components you need for most proposals.

As you design programs and services, you may decide you need to adjust your preconceived ideas to make them viable. This is a good thing. It is much better to adjust a design or redesign a project in the planning stages, before you implement it, rather than finding out at the end that your miscalculations caused an ineffective service or program and wasted people's time.

Below are some brief definitions for the core design elements. The following chapters explore each one in more detail, giving examples for different kinds of libraries, and illustrating their practical use in sample program designs. It's important to know that these terms are defined many different ways in various resources about planning. Planning sessions can derail when participants disagree about the use of these terms. Avoid this pitfall by agreeing to the definitions from the beginning. The definitions below are recommended because they lend themselves well to this method for planning effective library programs and services.

GOALS. Broad statements about the purpose of a program, project, or service. Goals generally state what you want to happen or expect as a result of offering a program or service in terms of the overall difference they will make for people. Goals must align with the library's mission and the goals in a library's strategic plan.

OBJECTIVES. State what you want to see happen as a result of the program or service in SMART (S = Specific, M = Measurable, A = Attainable, R = Realistic, T = Time-bound) terms. Use objectives to measure progress toward the goals.

OUTCOMES. The changes or benefits that result from offering the program or service. Usually outcomes are seen as differences in behavior, attitude, life status, or condition; or the acquisition of skills or knowledge.

ACTIVITIES. The steps that must be taken to accomplish the goals and reach the objectives and outcomes of your program, project, or service. Along with each activity, name the staff position that will perform the activity and the estimated amount of time it will take each position to complete each activity. This information can also be called a strategy or methodology.

TIME LINE. Illustrates the main activities required to complete a project, program, or service in chronological order.

BUDGET. Estimates the cost of a project, program, or service. Often it is divided into a personnel budget and a non-personnel budget. Total project cost equals the sum of the two budgets.

EVALUATION PLAN. Provides a method for measuring the effectiveness or success of a program, project, or service based on the degree to which the stated objectives and outcomes were accomplished.

What happens if you don't design a program using these elements, or something similar? You might think that because you've implemented many programs in the past, you already know how to do this without going to so much trouble. This might seem like overkill to you, and you are sure you can skip this step and get on with it. It is possible that you are already using this way of planning or thinking without knowing it. You may be working the steps in a different order, or from a different perspective. Maybe you call elements by different names because you have extensive advanced experience planning this way. If this is the case, it is possible you are doing just fine without learning this method. However, it is more likely that you haven't ever tried this kind of planning. Try it. Start with a simple project. You might be pleasantly surprised. Below is one example of what can happen when you don't design a program because you think you already know what you are doing, or because you've always done it one way because it has always worked.

The headline reads, "Librarian Wants to Ban 5-time Reading Champ from Contest," and the article tells the story of a library director in upstate New York who wants to ban a nine-year-old boy from the summer reading program because he has won it five years in a row and "hogs" it for himself (Stump 2013). This is not good for the boy; for the library, for libraries, or for librarians; for summer reading programs everywhere; for the community; or for parents. How did this happen? Possibly it happened because the purpose or goals of the summer reading program were not designed to align with the library's mission. Maybe the objectives did not measure the degree to which the goal was reached. Or, possibly, this summer reading program was offered year in and year out without much thought to program design, including goals and objectives. It is difficult to imagine what the goal was when one objective appears to be for children to read as many books as possible over the summer. Could the library's mission be to create speed-readers?

Unfortunately, when programs don't have goals that make sense, the likelihood this kind of thing will happen is fairly high. Participants and their parents perceived the program as a competition where the child who read the most books won. This perception was not an accident. It arose from the way the program was designed (or not) and promoted. Now the library director wants to change the rules to say the name of the winner will be pulled out of a hat. This program needs a good design, not a new rule about determining the winner. Don't let this happen at your library. Take the time and put in the effort to create solid designs. If things don't go the way you expected them to, you can easily make changes that will directly affect the targeted areas of your program or service that need improvement.

Forming a Team

Program and service planning is a group activity. The best programs and services often emerge from ideas expressed by a wide range of people who see things from different perspectives. Include staff members, board members, employees, administrators, principals, faculty, students, community members, and other stakeholders on your planning committees. If you are in a large library, you might want to form different committees to plan programs and services for different population segments; if you are in a small library, you might need only one committee to plan all library programs and services. The only rule is to include a range of people who are representative of your community, university, corporation, or school. Whenever possible, include appropriate subject specialists, people from agencies working on similar issues, or people with expertise in technology when applicable. Customize planning teams to suit the needs you are meeting and the methods you might use to meet the needs.

Key Points

After you have conducted a needs assessment, analyzed the results, and prioritized needs, the next step is to design or plan programs and services to meet the prioritized needs.

This can be the most rewarding part of library work because you can plan how to make a difference for people.

- Plans offer a pathway to provide effective library programs and services.
- Plans minimize risk.
- Program and service designs align with the library's mission, they help meet needs, and they help make a difference for people.
- Plans tell you what you intend to accomplish, the steps you will take to provide programs or services, the staff needed to implement them, the resources needed, how much they will cost, how long it will take, and how to measure success.
- The potential for making a difference increases dramatically when you partner with other agencies and organizations.
- Be careful about adapting a new technology, product, tool, or innovation simply because it is a popular trend.
- Every program, project, or service design needs these basic elements: goals, objectives, outcomes, activities, time line, budget, and evaluation plan.
- Program and service planning is a group activity.

The following chapters cover the basic elements of a program design in some detail. As you think through these elements with a specific program or service in mind, you will have the advantage of seeing some pitfalls and troubleshooting them before the implementation stage. Your program or service will be less likely to fail, and if it does, you will know exactly where you can make improvements in the design. The next chapter covers developing goals, objectives, and outcomes for library services and programs.

References

Stump, Scott. 2013. "Librarian Wants to Ban 5-time Reading Champ from Contest." *Today Books*, August 20. http://www.today.com/books/librarian-wants-ban-5-time-reading-champ-contest-6C10960198.

Developing Goals, Objectives, and Outcomes

AS YOU LEARNED IN THE PREVIOUS CHAPTER, every program, project, or service design needs these core elements: goals, objectives, outcomes, activities, time line, budget, and evaluation plan. This chapter guides you through the first steps of establishing goals, generating ideas, and creating objectives that incorporate outcomes for a library program or service design. The library planning process differs from library to library, so you may need to adapt these steps to work within your process. The timing of tasks might vary, or how you define "goal" or "priority" might differ. Whether your library's plan specifies goals or "service responses" (Nelson), you will have what you need to generate program and service ideas, and create objectives that incorporate outcomes.

Understanding and Determining Program and Service Goals

A *goal* is a broad statement about the purpose of a program, project, or service. Goals generally state what you want to happen or expect as a result of offering a program or service in terms of the overall difference it will make for people. Simply put, a goal states the solution to the need or problem you want to address. The goals of a library service or program can be the same as the library's goals, or a subset of them. Minimally, goals for library projects, programs, or services must align with the library's mission, vision, and strategic goals. Begin by stating the needs the library plans to address in simple terms.

Needs Examples

- Seniors need access to current health information.
- Students need open study and learning spaces.
- Children need reading opportunities.
- Teachers need materials and resources to support their classes.
- Adults need literacy training and support.
- Unemployed people need resources and training to help them become employed.
- Researchers need access to current information wherever they are.
- People need a place to make things and the tools to make them.

Then create simple goals by stating the inverse of the needs.

Needs and Corresponding Goals Examples

Need: Seniors need access to current health information.
Goal: Provide seniors access to current health information.

Need: Students need open study and learning spaces.
Goal: Provide students with open study and learning spaces.

Need: Children need reading opportunities.
Goal: Provide children with reading opportunities.

Need: Teachers need materials and resources to support their instruction
Goal: Provide teachers with materials and resources to support their instruction.

Need: Adults need literacy improvement.
Goal: Provide adults materials, tools, training, and support for improving their literacy skills.

Need: Unemployed community members need the resources and training to become employed.
Goal: Provide unemployed people resources and training for becoming employed.

Need: Researchers need to access information where they are.
Goal: Provide researchers access to information where they are.

Need: People need a place to make things and the tools to make them.
Goal: Provide a place where people can make things and provide the tools they need to make them.

Then ensure that the goal statements are aligned with the library's vision, mission, and strategic goals. Do this right away, before you explore specific service, program, or project ideas. Spending valuable time and energy generating program ideas meant to accomplish goals that are not within the scope of the library's purpose makes no sense. If you are working with needs that were identified through a community needs assessment, and if your library's plan is designed to meet those needs according to the library's mission vision and goals, you should find that simple goal statements like the examples above are suitable.

The goals of the programs and services your library offers derive from the library's plan, and the plan is designed to meet community needs that are within the scope of the library's mission.

If, however, you find that your goals are not in agreement with the library's strategic direction, a disconnect has emerged somewhere along the way. Stop here and figure out why. Unfortunately, all too often libraries do not have strategic plans, or the plan is a generic template or another library's plan that has been minimally customized. Plans like these are not relevant to a specific community, people's real needs, or a particular library. If you are working in a library like this, you must start at the beginning by conducting a community needs assessment (see chapter 4). Without an assessment you will not know people's needs. If you don't know people's needs, you cannot make plans and establish goals to meet their needs. If you don't have goals, you won't know what programs, services, and projects to offer that will benefit your community. If you want to provide effective library programs and services, you must first assess needs, then plan.

Librarians who are not in touch with their community's needs and those who work in libraries with outdated, insubstantial, or nonexistent strategic plans will have a difficult time establishing needs and goals. They often do whatever comes to mind, create projects they personally like or offer something they would like to learn about themselves, replicate another library's successful programs, or continue doing what they have always done. Some librarians continue to do the same things over and over because they think librarians have always done those things, and they are convinced that these programs and services have always worked. Sometimes librarians think they intuitively "know" the community's needs and the library's priorities without a needs assessment or plan. This is dangerous thinking. Communities and their needs are changing constantly. Libraries have gone though a monumental transformation in recent years, and their role or purpose is in constant flux. Under such dynamic circumstances, no librarian can "know" these things without doing the hard work of continuous assessment and planning.

Clifford A. Lynch observes, "To thrive in 2020, libraries need to make a ferocious and sustained shift in focus from collections to users" (Fontichiaro 2013). This indicates that some librarians were still focused on collections as late as 2013! Librarians who have not changed with the times may attempt to compensate by offering programs and services that they think all libraries are "supposed" to offer. Others may follow the latest fads because this gives them a false sense of direction. These approaches do not usually address the underlying problems or community needs. You cannot provide effective library programs and services without determining current community needs and undergoing the strategic planning process.

It is not unusual for librarians to have ideas for new programs, only to discover that the strategic plan has plotted a different course for the library. This can happen if a librarian has not been involved in the planning process, or if she has not made an effort to familiarize herself with the community's current information, educational, or recreational needs. Some librarians may not even be aware of the concept that community needs drive programs and services. It is never too late to shift your thinking.

Ideally, your library has already identified needs, conducted a strategic planning process, and determined the library's priorities or goals for a specified period of time. If you are fortunate enough to work in such a library, the plan will tell you all you need to know to move forward with program and service planning. Your library's vision and mission will be in place; a needs assessment will have been conducted; the data from your needs assessment will have been analyzed and synthesized; the needs determined; and the library's priorities or strategic goals set to accomplish the priorities for the next few years. Before you can consider what programs or services to offer or improve, or what new projects to initiate, refer to the strategic plan for guidance.

ⓖ Generating Program, Project, and Service Ideas

The next step is to generate specific program or service ideas that will help the library reach its strategic goals. Determine the best time to generate project ideas that will inform the library's plan. Again, this will differ from library to library depending on your planning method. It could be during or after the strategic planning process or separate from it altogether. It might be a formal process involving paperwork, or a less formal method like brainstorming. If your library is small, your director is flexible, or you are a one-person library, you may be able to introduce new project ideas at any time. Regardless of the timing or method you use, project ideas must align with the library's plan.

Some strategic plans are very specific about the programs and services the library will offer, and when, in the next three to five years. In these cases, the planning team has already been charged with generating ideas. Directors at these libraries may be resistant to new ideas for the next three to five years, so you cannot randomly show up in their offices with new project ideas. In this case, if you want to participate in generating ideas, find out when the next strategic planning will take place and request to be a participant. Make sure you understand the planning process at your library and your director's style before you forge ahead.

Brainstorming

One way to generate ideas for potential programs, projects, and services is to convene a team to brainstorm ways for the library to reach its goals. The makeup of the team will depend on the size of the library and the nature of the prioritized needs. For instance, if you work in a large library, and the community's most pressing need is for employment information and assistance, you would likely convene a brainstorming team on this single issue and include the adult services librarian, technology librarian, and an instruction librarian. You might also invite a local business leader, a representative from the unemployment office, an unemployed person, and a librarian from another library that is currently offering similar services or programs.

If you work in an academic institution where college students' most pressing information need is gaining skills to evaluate information, it might make sense to include a faculty member who teaches freshman English, a college student, and the instruction librarian. If you are in a corporate library that has prioritized meeting a need for accessing current information by employees, corporate officers, researchers, and field representatives, include on the team someone from each segment of the population you serve. You cannot know every person's need or every possible solution from all perspectives. A diverse team will offer valuable information to represent different points of view.

As is the case with most group planning activities, you will need a facilitator to lead the brainstorming process and a recorder to record the ideas. For the best results, they must not be participants in the brainstorming activities. It is very difficult to participate and lead or record at the same time, as these are different modes of operating. First inform the team about the library's vision, mission, and strategic goals; and the needs and program or service goals you have already determined. To stay focused and organized, the team should consider one need and goal at a time.

If you want to prompt the most creative ideas, don't put limits on the group or restrict their thinking. Brainstorming encourages a free exchange of creative ideas. When you have restrictions or rules for what kinds of ideas are acceptable, for instance, you inhibit creativity. Avoid any form of discouragement or blocking of ideas. Some standard ground rules for brainstorming include:

- Quantity over quality
- Encourage creativity
- Build on others' ideas
- One person speaks at a time
- Defer judging or criticizing others' ideas
- Discuss and clarify later

Aim for as many creative ideas as possible. Don't limit yourselves to ideas that have been thought out thoroughly or already proven. Fruitful idea-generating exercises encourage building on the ideas of others. Encourage participants spontaneously to offer ideas for next steps for developing another person's idea. Explain how building on others' ideas is a good thing rather than "stealing" another's idea. Suggest that anyone who is building on another's idea acknowledge the other person before he elaborates. Criticizing or judging someone's creative idea or interrupting while someone else is expressing an idea will stop free thinking. Explain that the ideas will be discussed and clarified later, because when you stop brainstorming to discuss the details of one idea, you stop the free flow of new ideas. When you allow this to happen, people forget they are supposed to be brainstorming. Keep people thinking in their right brains. Brainstorming done poorly is a frustrating experience for everyone involved.

If you know another way to generate creative ideas or to brainstorm more effectively, by all means employ the method that works best for you. Try alternative methods such as online brainstorming, written approaches, or mind mapping. (Mind mapping is a visual way to organize ideas and concepts.) In her article "4 Steps to Effective Brainstorming," Susan Adams cites a method developed by Ralph Keeney of Duke University that suggests brainstorming is more effective when before participants start they are clear about the objectives they hope to achieve. This approach of thinking "inside" the box helps to keep people focused on viable solutions. Providing team members with the needs and goals along with clear objectives could lead fairly quickly to some very useful ideas that don't need a great deal of extra work later on. Keeney contends that when participants come to a meeting with solutions, they are less likely to be distracted by one person's idea or forget to address multiple objectives (Adams 2013).

Once everyone understands the brainstorming process you are using, it will get easier. In fact, as people become familiar with the logic of the brainstorming method, they tend to think through the first few steps on their own before sharing their ideas with the group. This usually weeds out ideas that are not in line with the library's mission, vision, and goals before people say them.

PROGRAM IDEA EXAMPLES

Continuing to build using the need/goal examples listed above, corresponding program, service, and project ideas that a brainstorming session might yield are listed below:

Need: Seniors need access to current health information.
Goal: Provide seniors access to current health information.
Program/Service/Project Ideas:

1. Computer instruction on using medical websites and databases including how to evaluate health information
2. Consumer health collection of print materials
3. Library Web portal with links to health information websites

Need: Students need open study and learning spaces.
Goal: Provide students with open study and learning spaces.
Program/Service/Project Ideas:

1. Create more open/working spaces in teen area
2. Convert a meeting room to an open study space
3. Build an addition to make a learning commons

Need: Researchers need to access information where they are.
Goal: Provide researchers access to information where they are.
Program/Service/Project Ideas:

1. Online portal that provides access points for researchers
2. App for delivering current information to mobile devices
3. Cloud computing services

Exercise

List some program/service/project ideas for the following needs/goals:

Need: Children need reading opportunities.
Goal: Provide children with reading opportunities.

Need: Teachers need materials and resources to support their instruction.
Goal: Provide teachers with materials and resources to support their instruction.

Need: Adults need literacy improvement.
Goal: Provide adults materials, tools, training, and support for improving their literacy skills.

Need: Unemployed community members need the resources and training to become employed.
Goal: Provide unemployed people resources and training for becoming employed.

Need: People need a place to make things and the tools to make them.
Goal: Provide a place where people can make things and provide the tools they need to make them.

⊚ Creating Objectives and Incorporating Outcomes

OBJECTIVES. State what you want to see happen as a result of the program or service in SMART (S = Specific, M = Measurable, A = Attainable, R = Realistic, T = Time-bound) terms. Use objectives to measure progress toward the goals.

OUTCOMES. State the changes or benefits that happen for people as a result of offering the program or service. Usually outcomes are seen as differences in behavior, attitude, life status, or condition; or the acquisition of skills or knowledge.

Once you have program or service goals for meeting a specific need, and viable ideas for how to reach the goal, you are ready to create objectives for the program or service idea. This is when a program design really starts to take shape. Make objectives that are **S**pecific, **M**easurable, **A**chievable, **R**ealistic, and **T**ime-bound (SMART) to indicate the results you expect. Objectives are the indicators for measuring the success of your efforts. By stating the objectives clearly and incorporating them into the program design from the start, you can determine more easily the activities you need to perform to achieve the results you expect. In addition, clear objectives stated in SMART terms will show you how to evaluate the program, project, or service in the end. Objectives are the roadmap for your project design. Continuing to build on Progrm Idea Example 1 on page 80, here are some possible program objectives:

Need: Seniors need access to current health information.

Goal: Provide seniors access to current health information.

Program/Service/Project Idea: Computer instruction on using medical websites and databases including how to evaluate health information.

Objectives:

1. By December 2015, 75 percent of the seniors who completed computer classes on using medical websites and databases will say they are more knowledgeable about accessing current health information online and how to evaluate it.
2. By December 2015, 80 percent of seniors who completed classes will say their ability to access current health information has helped them make informed health-related decisions.
3. By July 2015, 90 percent of participants will say they are more confident using computers to access health information.
4. By December 2015, 40 percent of seniors participating will say they used the library's medical web portal to find current health information.

Incorporating Outcomes

Effective programs and services have objectives that are constructed around meaningful outcomes for people. Outcomes reflect changes in behavior, attitude, life status, or condition; or the acquisition of skills or knowledge. First ask how people will benefit from the program or service, and then build your answer into the program's objectives. For instance, using the example above, it is a clear indicator of the program's success that as a result of participating, seniors will know more about how to access and evaluate medical information. A successful program will result in seniors who know more about using library resources to make informed health decisions, give them more confidence in accessing health information, and prompt more seniors to use the library's medical website to find health information.

Making SMART objectives that incorporate outcomes for people may be a new concept for some librarians, primarily because most librarians have been taught to measure their success by counting things. This notion is reinforced when school administrators, town officials, academic deans, and corporate headquarters ask for statistics to establish the library's worth or measure your performance. Historically, we have seen a disconnect between the purpose of libraries and the methods we use for measuring our effectiveness. Unfortunately, this has put librarians at a disadvantage when it comes to coping with rapid change and proving our worth in difficult economies. When you focus on making a difference for people, it is easier to navigate change.

Large numbers of class participants or program attendees, high circulation statistics, head counts, or website hits tell you nothing about the effectiveness of a program or service. Increasing numbers is no indicator of the difference a program or service has made for people. Make objectives that indicate a community need has been met to the satisfaction of a program's goal. Avoid objectives that aim for higher numbers or increased statistics alone.

Recently, in an effort to stay relevant and attract new users, some libraries have morphed into community centers, video gaming havens, "destinations," and maker-spaces. The purpose or role of these libraries may be primarily as catalysts to spark community enthusiasm, "centers of discovery," or "communication-places" (Nikitin and Jackson 2009). In libraries where the goal is to attract people or provide a place for people to gather, counting numbers is a valid way to evaluate their success. On the other hand, libraries that exist as information centers to promote reading, literacy, education, and provide activities that support the betterment of a community in this regard should avoid objectives that strive for increasing statistics as an indicator of success. The underlying key to the objectives is in the library's purpose. Ask what your library is trying to accomplish.

Pitfalls: A Case Study

Once you understand the importance of having goals and objectives for programs and services that relate directly to community needs and the library's mission, vision, and purpose, you will see how easily things can go wrong when these elements aren't in place. Consider the example of the library where the director changed the summer reading program rules because one child read "too many" books (see chapter 6). What was the program's goal? What were the objectives? Why were children reading as many books as they could over the summer if not to help the library reach a goal?

In public libraries across the United States, librarians routinely hold summer reading programs. Do most librarians who run summer reading programs know the goals and objectives of their programs? The goals of summer reading programs for New York State libraries are listed below (New York State Library 2013).

- Advance literacy and academic performance by engaging children and teens in reading and reading-related activities during the summer months.
- Foster a love of reading through public library programs and services.
- Increase successful reading experiences through librarian-supported, self-selected, voluntary reading.
- Involve parents and all family members in the library summer reading experience.
- Improve children's access to library materials and activities, which will encourage them to become lifelong library users.
- Increase the number of children and teens participating in public library summer reading programs.

What are some SMART objectives that might indicate a program reached its goal of advancing literacy and academic programs, fostering a love of reading, increasing successful reading experiences, involving parents and family members, or improving a child's access to library materials? Here are some possibilities:

1. School test scores show that 85 percent of participants advanced their academic performance and literacy by the beginning of the 2015–2016 school year.
2. Seventy-five percent of participants will say it is easier to access library materials and activities as a result of the summer reading program.
3. Fifty percent of participants' family members will be involved in the summer reading program.
4. Seventy percent of participants will say their love of reading has increased due to the summer reading program.

Would conducting a contest to determine which child read the most books be the best way to measure the success of a reading program? Would counting the total number of books read over the summer tell you if the program advanced literacy and academic programs, fostered a love of reading, increased successful reading experiences, involved parents and family members, or improved a child's access to library materials? What will increasing the number of participants indicate? This is only one example, meant to help you think through the process of effective program design. In the end, you want to meet your community's needs, not create a community upheaval and negative national news coverage for your library. Avoid this trap by creating program objectives that are related to the goals.

⑥ Partnering and Collaborating

Including leaders from other organizations in your community, department heads from other village, academic, or corporate departments, and local business leaders and innovators in this process offers a real advantage. Other agencies, departments, or businesses may be providing similar programs or services, others may be thinking about providing them, and people who have expertise could help you meet community needs. How often have you or someone on your staff had a program idea, only to be met with responses such as, "We don't have the expertise," "We don't have the money," or "That idea is too big for our little library to accomplish"? By partnering and collaborating with others, your library can do much more than it could possibly do on its own. You can make a bigger difference when you work with others because you can share the responsibilities, funding, expertise, and resources. Together you can provide more effective, consistent, and holistic services to the community at large.

◎ Using Needs, Goals, and Program Ideas to Stay On Track

Knowing your community's needs, the corresponding goals and program ideas, along with the library's mission, role, and purpose will help keep the library on track. When you have the information about needs that can come only from analyzing an assessment, you will know how to select the programs and services that are "right" for the library and community. All you do will lead the library in the direction of accomplishing meaningful goals that will make a difference for people. When staff are focused in the same direction with a common purpose, you are less likely to get distracted. It will be difficult to establish and implement services and programs that are not relevant to your particular community when everyone is on the same page. You will be amazed at all you can accomplish when you are all working together in the same direction.

Suppose your community needs a playground, and a community member approaches the public library where you work about donating funds to install play equipment outside the library. The goal of this project would be to provide a play area for children. Is this within the scope of the library's vision, mission, and goals? Does the library's strategic plan identify building a playground as a top priority in the next three to five years? Is the library's role to provide recreational equipment for the community? If the answer is "yes," then this would be a welcome donation; however, when the answer is "no" you are obligated to thank the potential donor for the kind offer and redirect her to the entity in your town that is responsible for playgrounds. Alternatively, you might tell her what the library does have planned and convince her to donate funds for one of those programs, projects, or services.

In another scenario, your library's friends' group is very enthusiastic, and the new president has extensive fund-raising experience. This gives your library a real advantage because funding has been shrinking, the budget is tight, and no one on your staff has significant fund-raising experience. Without consulting the library director, the friends' president has launched a fund-raising campaign for building an addition onto the library. Although the library is on the small side and it would be nice to have some extra space, this is not within the scope of the library's current plans. The planning team has determined some priorities that include establishing reference service, hiring a professional librarian, and contracting with a technology company to update the mostly nonfunctional computers. More space for the library is not a priority at this time.

When you are clear about the needs your library plans to meet and how you will meet them, you will know when to say "yes" and when to say "no." If you aren't too sure about the community's real needs or how to go about meeting them, accepting a donation for a playground or funds for a library addition might seem like a harmless gesture. Implementing these projects will take staff time, funds will need to be administered, the areas will need to be monitored, new staff hired and supervised, and legal concerns and liability issues may be involved. This all takes away time, money, resources, and effort from accomplishing what the library must do to meet the prioritized needs. It can be very difficult to turn away a donation for something that is needed or perceived as needed in the community at large; however, the library has a role, vision, mission and goals, programs and services for a reason. One big reason is to keep the library on track and to guide library staff in doing the work they were hired to do. Libraries cannot be everything to everyone. Your staff time, energy, and money are more efficiently used when you have goals and program ideas meant to meet community needs.

◎ Key Points

This chapter explained the first steps of establishing goals, generating ideas, and creating objectives that incorporate outcomes for library program or service designs. Now you have an understanding of the first three core elements of an effective program or service design: goals, objectives, and outcomes.

- Goals for library projects, programs, or services must align with the library's mission, vision, and strategic goals.
- Begin by stating the needs the library plans to address.
- Next, create goals by stating the inverse of the needs.
- Then convene a diverse team to generate creative program or service ideas that will help the library reach its goals.
- Make objectives that are **S**pecific, **M**easurable, **A**chievable, **R**ealistic and **T**ime-bound (SMART) to indicate the results you expect from a program or service.
- Effective programs and services have objectives that are constructed around meaningful outcomes for people.
- You can make a bigger difference when you collaborate with others because you can share the responsibilities, funding, expertise, and resources.

The next chapters will cover the remaining elements in effective program and service design: activities, time line, budget, and evaluation plan.

◎ References

Adams, Susan. 2013. *4 Steps to Successful Brainstorming*, March 5. http://www.forbes.com/sites/susanadams/2013/03/05/4-steps-to-successful-brainstorming/.

Fontichiaro, Kristin. 2013. In *Library 2020: Today's Leading Visionaries Describe Tomorrow's Library*, edited by Joseph Janes, 7–13. Lanham, MD: Scarecrow Press.

Nelson, Sandra. 2008. *Strategic Planning for Results*. Chicago: American Library Association.

New York State Library. 2013. "Summer Reading at New York Libraries," April 24. http://www.nysl.nysed.gov/libdev/summer/research.htm.

Nikitin, Cynthia, and Josh Jackson. 2009. *Libraries that Matter*, January 2. https://www.pps.org/reference/librariesthatmatter-2/.

CHAPTER 8

Determining Activities, Staff Requirements, and Time Line

NOW YOU HAVE A PROGRAM OR SERVICE IDEA that has a goal and SMART objectives that address specific outcomes. You understand that you must design library programs and services to help the library move forward by meeting the needs of the people in your community—whether they are residents in a town, city, or village; students and faculty at a university or college; employees of a corporation or agency; or teachers and students in a school. You and your staff have determined that the goal and objectives of your program or service align with the library's vision, mission, and strategic direction.

As you learned in chapter 6, designing effective programs and services may involve many people, including library staff, stakeholders, partners and collaborators, the strategic planning committee, board members, and possibly volunteers from the community. This depends on your library, its size, and organizational structure. There is no one formula to follow. It is important to work within the existing structure of your organization, so you don't overstep boundaries, alienate people, and drive the process into a ditch. Program leaders, service leaders, committee chairs, and project managers are still responsible for convening teams and committees, and leading productive meetings that include developing goals, objectives, outcomes, action items, assigning tasks, and ensuring accountability for the success of their programs, services, and projects. This is no different from the way you usually work. Focusing on people and planning programs to meet their needs might be a different paradigm for you and your staff. The degree of thought you will give to the elements of program and service design will increase; however, you should be able to make these changes easily within your existing organizational structure and management style.

Defining Program and Service Activities

The next step is to determine the activities or action steps necessary to establish the service or implement the program. This is the heart of your program or service design. At this stage you are deciding how your program or service will function or operate. This is your chance to be creative and innovative, and to significantly influence the evolving role of your library. This is a great opportunity for librarians to lead change in their communities and set an example for others in our field.

Remember, you can reach a goal, accomplish objectives, and ensure outcomes multiple ways. So, too, you can outline program activities many ways. Activities define the work that must be done to accomplish the objectives of a program or service. Ask, "What are the tasks we must we do to complete the project or implement the service?" Formulate the activities so that you can easily verify their completion. The status of each activity needs to be determined easily every step along the way. Activities must have a definite beginning and end; and each activity must comprise a work assignment that is manageable and independent of other work activities. Most activities must be completed in a defined sequence, so list the activities in chronological order for easy tracking. For example, suppose your program idea is to provide a 3-D printer, design software, and instruction on how to use the software and printer in your library's makerspace. A sample preliminary activity list might look like the one on the following page.

Sample Preliminary Activities List for Makerspace

- Investigate 3-D printer options
- Investigate software options
- Assess capability of current computers to run hardware and software
- Select software
- Select 3-D printer
- Select furniture for printer, instruction, and additional workspace
- Prepare purchase order for 3-D printer, software, and furniture
- Purchase 3-D printer, software, and furniture
- Purchase necessary upgrades for computers
- Upgrade computers to handle the software and 3-D printer
- Set up 3-D printer
- Install software
- Provide training for library staff on how to use software and 3-D printer
- Create policies, guidelines for 3-D printer use
- Design classes to teach using software and 3-D printer
- Schedule makerspace for teaching classes

DEFINING PROGRAM ACTIVITIES EXERCISE

In the space below, make a preliminary list of the activities that must be completed to implement the following program. Change or adjust the goal and/or objectives, if necessary, using the information you learned in chapter 7:

_____
_____
_____
_____
_____

Program Title: Enabling Healthy Choices: Teaching Seniors To Use Technology to Find and Evaluate Medical Information

Goal: Provide seniors the information and knowledge they need to access current and reliable online health information.

Objectives:

1. By December 2015, 75 percent of the seniors who completed computer classes on finding/using medical websites and evaluating them will say they are more knowledgeable about accessing current health information online and how to evaluate it.

2. By December 2015, 80 percent of seniors will say their ability to access current health information has helped them make more informed health-related decisions.

3. By December 2015, 75 percent of participants will say they have used the information they learned to answer their own health-related questions.

4. By July 2015, 90 percent of participants will say they are more confident using computers to find and access health information.

5. By December 2015, 40 percent of seniors will say they used the library's medical Web portal to access current health information.

List possible program activities in chronological order:

_____   _____
_____   _____
_____   _____
_____   _____
_____   _____
_____   _____
_____   _____
_____   _____
_____   _____
_____   _____

What questions did you have about the project as you listed the activities?

As it developed, did the program design prompt you to adjust the goal or objectives? Explain.

_____

_____

_____

Did new program ideas occur to you as you listed the activities for this one?

_____

_____

_____

- Advertise classes
- Register people for classes
- Prepare instructional materials
- Teach classes on how to use software and 3-D printer
- Evaluate classes
- Provide ongoing support on software and 3-D printer use
- Weekly program team meetings

As you list the activities or action steps your program requires, you may discover that the idea you originally had in mind may not work in practice. This is OK. It is part of the process. Plan to rework your list, or add and subtract activities as you go. Keep going. Order the activities sequentially. Work on alternative ways to reach a goal, or adjust the goal so it is more realistic. Revise the objectives if you can see they are not achievable, or change the target dates if that makes more sense for the program's success. In the beginning you are working on a _preliminary_ activities list. It will change and develop as you go. Remain open to new ideas from others. Refine it and tweak it as necessary. During this stage an entirely new program idea may occur to you. Write it down for another day and continue working on your original idea. Stay focused. You might realize that the program you are planning is two or three programs, so break down the activities and work the lists accordingly. It is called _planning_ for a reason.

As you list each task that must be completed, you are making critical design decisions about how the program or service will "look." Defining activities is a single step in this logical planning process, yet it is the most dynamic and creative step. As you think about the activities of the program or service, you are developing the details of your original idea and designing the program as you go. Be innovative and think outside the box. Insert or create activities that you had not previously considered. Take chances on breaking new ground. Consider new partners or adding team members who have the expertise or skills required to perform certain program activities. Ask them to join the team or interview them. You are in "discovery mode."

Avoid barriers, obstructions, or negative thoughts such as "We don't have the money," "We don't have enough staff and everyone is already too busy," "We already tried that and it didn't work," "We don't have the experience or knowledge," or "We are just a small library and we can only implement small programs." These are words some librarians repeat when the going gets tough or they fear failure. Some librarians who dislike change or think that designing new programs and services is too difficult will say these things to derail the process. Do not let them get in your way. Designing effective programs and services means change. Change is not easy. But libraries today are in a constant state of dynamic change—like it or not. If you resist change now, your library will be left behind, and your community will surely suffer.

As you define the activities, your program or service design begins to take shape. Arrange the activities in chronological order as best you can. Keep reading through the activities for anything you may have missed. Insert additional activities as they become apparent to you. Remove inessential activities. Check your objectives to ensure that performing the activities will accomplish the objectives. Include activities necessary to evaluate the program, such as conducting surveys or informal interviews.

As is true with all of the steps in this process, it is best if you seek input from others who have knowledge or experience in the topic of the service or program you are designing. In general, when you ask people about activities they know about or how to do, you are more likely to end up with a relatively complete and accurate activity list that is realistic. Including others who might work on a program you are designing will encourage their buy-in. They are likely to become enthusiastic about what you are planning, and in the end they usually will work harder on a program that they have had a hand in designing.

This process is both creative and logical. Librarians who can easily alternate between creative thinking and logical thinking are likely to be comfortable with this process. It can be fun and challenging to exercise both kinds of thinking at once. For those who are not comfortable with this kind of thinking, the process accommodates all kinds of thinkers. Most people will find a place where they can be comfortable and contribute.

When you and your team members agree about what you are doing, you will accomplish more in less time. Conflicts about which programs and services to offer will be minimized. You are not making decisions based on personal preferences or what one staff member "wants" to do. Rather, you are making objective decisions about which activities to do based on the facts about your community and following a logical planning process. This diminishes any imbalance you may have experienced in the past that was created by those people with more power and authority or those who resisted change, for example.

Remember to customize the program or service design to your community and don't revert to replicating what you or other libraries have done in the past. What the people in your community, college or university, school, or business need differs from what people in other communities, colleges or universities, schools or businesses need. What they need now is different from what they needed five years ago. Be realistic. Sometimes this means designing a model or pilot program to pave the way for a larger or more complex idea in the future.

Doing the Research

If your program idea or something similar has already been implemented elsewhere, researching the "lessons learned" by others will benefit your program or service design.

Many library and information science best practices can guide you in this process. For instance, consumer health best practices in public libraries include the following from the Delaware Division of Libraries (2015, 5):

- Form strategic partnerships that include public libraries, medical libraries, and community organizations and agencies.
- Assess community needs and plan the scope of service.
- Provide consumer health information at the time of need and at the point of service.
- Offer current, reliable, and accurate sources of information.
- Promote and market the service widely.
- Develop plans to sustain and/or expand the service.

These best practices were developed as a result of the experiences of others who had implemented consumer health programs in public libraries. It makes sense to follow these guidelines versus starting from scratch as if no one else has gone before you. This increases the chances your program will be successful and reduces your chances for failure.

Research other similar programs to find out the pitfalls to avoid. Build on the success of others. Don't duplicate other programs designed for other communities or populations; instead, adapt the successful aspects of other programs to enhance your design. Don't limit your research strictly to library programs and services. For instance, the Makerspace Playbook (2015) available from Makerspace.com provides best practices and tips on how to establish and start up a makerspace in different kinds of locations; however, it applies to libraries.

Involve your partners and collaborators in defining activities that relate to their work on the project. For instance, some public libraries have programs that involve nurses and social workers in the library. These partners from the nursing and social work fields are the ones to define the program activities that relate to accomplishing specific program goals.

Review the Literature

Refer to recent issues of library journals and magazines to see what is currently happening in other libraries relevant to your program or service idea. Take the lead from those who have gone before you. This does not mean to copy what others have done. Your program must be designed to meet the needs of your community; however, you can always learn from the many innovative and creative programs constantly being implemented in libraries. For example, in the July 2014 issue of *School Library Journal*, Sarah Bayliss described various library music programs that support early learning. This article is full of useful information about specific programs, resources for research, tips from librarians who have implemented music programs for young children, and best practices from leaders in the field. In the same issue of *School Library Journal*, Lauren Barak wrote about programs for people with autism. You don't have to look far for literature on library programs and services of all kinds.

If you are planning a makerspace, you are at an advantage because many makerspaces have been in operation for a few years. Makerspaces have been around in libraries since about 2011, and they also exist in schools and museums. An abundance of literature about different makerspace approaches includes what went right and what went wrong in different environments. By learning from the experiences of others, you can create a more successful makerspace. This is true for all kinds of programs and services in all types of libraries.

If you use books for your research, supplement the information they contain with current periodical literature or stories in online posts, blogs, and discussion lists.

Interviews

Contact the librarians who were involved if you have questions about a specific program or service they planned and implemented. If a specific program or service you read or learn about looks especially interesting to you, or it is similar to what you are planning, ask the librarians who led it if they are willing to share their experiences. If they are receptive, prepare a set of informed questions in advance and make a phone appointment. Make sure you are organized. You want to use their time wisely. In general, librarians are generous with information and eager to share information about their innovative programs and services. Librarians are in the information-sharing business.

Interview nonlibrarians who have experience implementing programs like yours. For instance, many schools and nonprofits have successful makerspaces. Communicate with experts in the field who have the knowledge and expertise to steer you in the right direction. They may be able to answer your questions or refer you to someone who can. Your literature review has likely led you to some names of people who are well respected and knowledgeable in their fields.

Field Trips

If you live near an innovative program or service that you might want to model yours after, visit it. Make an appointment in advance with the coordinator and arrive with questions to ask. Ask what they did to make it successful. Ask if they would do anything differently. Observe the program or service in action. Take notes.

Continuing Education

Inform yourself about the topic or subject area, especially if it is new territory for you. You don't want to overlook an important step or activity that your program or service requires. Many webinars and continuing education opportunities are available about topics relating to library programs and services. Some are free. Begin with a library association that might be likely to have training or education on your topic. For instance, if you were planning a consumer health information program, the National Network of Libraries of Medicine (NN/LM) in your region would be a good place to start. Many state library agencies provide continuing education opportunities for librarians in their state. Some states open webinars and tutorials to people both inside and outside their states.

WebJunction (http://www.webjunction.org/events/webjunction.html) offers webinars on a wide variety of topics related to library programs and services.

TechSoup (https://techsoupforlibraries.org/events) offers webinars for librarians on technology-related topics.

The Public Library Association (http://www.ala.org/pla/onlinelearning/webinars/ondemand) offers continuing education on topics related to public libraries.

The National Network of Libraries of Medicine (http://nnlm.gov/scr/training/) offers continuing education on health and medical information subjects.

These are only a few examples. Some webinars are archived for future use, so you can view or listen to them at your convenience.

Doing the research shows you how to prevent avoidable mistakes. By doing the research, you can be "smart" about using available resources and spending funds wisely. When you take the time to do the research, you demonstrate that you are a team player who communicates and shares knowledge with others in your profession for the betterment of your community. Informing yourself about best practices helps promote the value of libraries and the status of our profession. It gives you the information you need and the confidence to "sell" your idea if you need additional funding. Research shows others you know what you are talking about. Adjust the activities for your program to reflect any changes you are making in your program design as a result of what you learn by doing the research.

Determining Who Will Do the Work and How Long It Will Take

When you are confident that your activities list is complete, then you are ready to determine who will do the work and estimate how long it will take them to perform each task. Start by assigning each activity to a staff position or consultant position. Although it is tempting to associate a specific staff member with each activity, it is important to stay as objective as possible at this point by completing this step on the position level. Positions usually remain in place, whereas staff members may change jobs or leave. If you plan a program or service around specific staff members, you may need to go back to the drawing board if things change. By assigning activities to positions you will reduce the variables, thus making this step easier in the long run. If you have a question about which position should perform a task, refer to the position descriptions to make this decision. Ask the library director, personnel office, human resources librarian, or the person who handles employment matters in your town or organization.

Your approach will depend on your work culture, your position, and your interpersonal communication skills. Ideally, all library staff members have been involved in the library's planning process. They are all "on board" about the library's strategic direction, program, and service priorities, and they were part of a team that suggested the specific program or service you are currently planning. You have included interested staff members, partners, people with expertise and skills related to the program, and other stakeholders on the program planning team. These people are looking forward to providing new effective programs and services, and they welcome the opportunity to be involved.

It is best if you are the library director or programming librarian, or have some authority in the areas of program and service development and implementation. If this sounds like your situation, this step will be fairly easy. Involve staff and seek their input. When you show people you are open to what they have to say, it will give them ownership in the program or service. Ownership contributes to the overall success of programs and services.

Verify with each person in the positions to which you have assigned an activity that their position is the right one for the job. They may have a different view on which position should do the work. Listen to them. If their position is not the appropriate one, they probably will be able to tell you which one is. Make any necessary adjustments to the staff assignments on your preliminary activities list based on their input. Because the people in the positions likely to do the work probably have prior experience with doing similar tasks, they are the best qualified for estimating time requirements. Ask these people to estimate how long it might take them to do each task. Add columns to your activities list for 1) what position will do the work and 2) how long it will take, as shown in table 8.1.

Table 8.1. Estimated Time To Perform Tasks Examples

TASK	POSITION	TIME
Investigate 3-D printer and software options	Technology Librarian	10 hours
Select software and 3-D printer	Technology Librarian	1 hour
Purchase the software and 3-D printer	Administrative Assistant	1 hour

Assign tasks that do not fall within the scope of work for any existing library or partner position to a consultant or a position outside the library. All tasks must be assigned to a position. Someone must do every task. If activities have no one to do them, your program will not be successful. Always include someone to manage the program or service and include administrative support. Include all of these tasks on the activities list. When estimating time, make sure you allow for meetings, reporting, communications, curriculum design, evaluation, and other activities that are critical to the project's success.

In work environments where staff members are not involved in planning, approaching people about their job duties, mentioning possible new tasks, asking how long the tasks might take to perform, or introducing the idea of a new program or service may not be well received. People may become defensive or threatened when you mention what they perceive as "new work." They may think you are about to give them more work when they already feel overworked. Bad experiences from the past may have taught them that new programs and services means more work for them, and they are not interested.

Put yourself in their position. Make it clear that you are in the *planning* stage and you are working on a *preliminary* activities list for a *proposed* program or service. Explain that the program or service is in the library's plan and is meant to meet community needs. A new program does not mean they will have more work to do. Tell them that they might have the opportunity to do different work to help implement a new service; however, in that case some of their current tasks will be delegated to another staff member to free up the necessary time.

Be aware of your library's culture before you approach staff. Some work environments are not open to creative thinking. Developing innovative library services and programs is a foreign concept that may threaten some or make others uncomfortable. They can sense change, and change is their enemy. Ultimately, use your best judgment about whether to involve staff at this stage; however, it is very difficult to provide effective programs and services without a fully engaged staff.

As you learned in chapter 6, it is important to involve staff and other stakeholders in the planning process from the start. If you get to this stage and find a degree of resistance that might threaten the success of the program or service, you may have work to do in terms of involving staff in the strategic planning process; however, this should not stop you. Go back to the strategic planning process and involve staff. Learn from this oversight; don't force the issue.

Creating a Time Line

Time lines are visual tools that help you design and manage a program or implement a service. They illustrate all of the activities in chronological order, who is responsible for each task, and when each task will be performed. Now that you have all of this information, you are ready to create a time line. Time lines have many variations; table 8.2 shows one example.

Table 8.2. Makerspace Time Line Example

ACTIVITY	STAFF	JAN	FEB	MAR	APR	MAY	JUNE	JUL
Investigate 3-D printer and software options	TL	√						
Select software and 3-D printer	TL	√						
Purchase the software and 3-D printer	AA	√						
Upgrade makerspace computers	TL		√					
Set up printer	TL		√					
Install software	TL		√					
Create policies, guidelines for 3-D printer use	TL		√					
Design classes to teach software and 3-D printer	TL, IL			√				
Prepare instructional materials	IL, PL			√				
Train makerspace staff how to use software and 3-D printer	TL, IL				√			
Schedule makerspace for teaching classes to public	PL, AA				√			
Advertise classes for public	PL, AA				√	√		
Register people for classes	AA				√	√		
Teach public classes on how to use software and 3-D printer	IL					√	√	√
Evaluate classes	PL					√	√	√
Provide ongoing support for software and 3-D printer	PL, TL					√	√	√

AA = Administrative Assistant

PL = Program Librarian

TL = Technology Librarian

IL = Instruction Librarian

Complete the task column on the time line by recording the activities list in chronological order. Then indicate when each activity will occur relative to the duration of the project. Don't be concerned with the hours a task will take, but rather the day, week, or month in which it will be done. (You will work with the amount of time each task will take in the next chapter about budgets.) Think of the time line as an "at-a-glance" version of your program or service. It shows when an activity will start and when it will end, as well as which activities will overlap. You can see which activities must be completed before others begin.

A new service or program may require a time line for implementation only. Following implementation, a service or program may seem to run on "autopilot"; however, having time lines for ongoing services and programs can be very useful for library directors and program coordinators who usually manage multiple projects. Time lines document which staff members are involved in which program or service; they serve as reminders of staff members' responsibilities; they can be useful for performance evaluations, updating job descriptions, and determining a staff member's workload.

ⓖ Key Points

In this chapter you learned what is at the heart of effective program and service design. Defining the required activities in chronological order, which positions will perform the activities, when they will do the activities, and how long it will take them determines how the program or service will function or operate.

- Activities define the work that must be done to accomplish the objectives of a program or service.
- You can reach a goal, accomplish objectives, and ensure outcomes in multiple ways.
- Determining activities is the most dynamic and creative step in providing effective library services and programs.
- Be innovative and think outside the box. Take chances on breaking new ground.
- Seek input from others.
- Avoid barriers, obstructions, or negative thoughts.
- Providing effective programs and services to meet community needs means change.
- Customize the program or service design to your community.
- Be realistic.
- Researching experiences of others will benefit your program or service design.
- Inform yourself about the topic or subject area.
- Follow best practices.
- Be aware of your library's culture before you approach staff about new program or service activities.
- Determine who will do activities at the position level. All tasks must be assigned to a position.
- Time lines are visual tools that are useful in helping you design and manage a program or implement a service.

The next chapter will cover how to create a budget for your program or service. This will give you an understanding of the resources you need to implement your program or service.

ⓖ References

Barak, Lauren. 2014. "Bridging the Gap: Librarians are Making Services More Accessible for a Diverse Autistic Population." *School Library Journal* (July): 28+. *Information Science and Library Issues Collection.* GALE|A373034844 id=GALE%7CA373034844&v=2.1&u=nm_p_elportal&it=r&p=PPIS&sw=w&asid=9aea6d5f14eaca4fd490513924ba12b1.

Bayliss, Sarah. 2014. "Why Music Matters: Library Music Programs are Fun and Support Early Learning." *School Library Journal* (July): 20+. *Information Science and Library Issues Collection.* GALE|A373034842. id=GALE%7CA373034842&v=2.1&u=nm_p_elportal&it=r&p=PPIS&sw=w&asid=71102c6cb64ef37ca461041a1f3aef91.

Delaware Division of Libraries. 2015. "Consumer Health Information: Best Practices for Public Libraries." Accessed July 23, 2015. http://libraries.delaware.gov/planning/pdfs/ConsumerHealthBestracticesPublicLibraries.pdf.

Makerspace Playbook. 2015. Makerspace.com. Accessed July 23, 2015. http://makered.org/wp-content/uploads/2014/09/Makerspace-Playbook-Feb-2013.pdf.

CHAPTER 9

Creating a Program Budget

THE PREVIOUS CHAPTER COVERED HOW TO DEFINE effective program or service activities, how to identify who will do the activities, and how long it will take them to perform the activities. The next step is to create a budget for the program or service you are planning. One of the most important aspects of planning programs and services is allocating adequate resources. For a program or service to be successful and effective, sufficient resources must be allocated to implement and support it. Resources are not just money. Resources are the people, equipment, supplies, materials, and space your program requires. First, you must determine all the resources that are necessary to implement and support a program or service; then, attach a cost to them, seek them out, or get them funded. Because you are still planning, you may want to adjust program activities or costs as you develop the budget.

Developing the Budget

Developing a budget for your program or service and allocating resources necessary for implementation comes relatively late in the planning process. It is important to the integrity of the process covered in this book to understand why this is. The only way to determine the cost of a program or service is to first know the program's goal and objectives, what you want to accomplish in terms of outcomes for people, and the details of how it will be implemented and supported. You must know the activities; personnel (who is going to do what and how long it will take them); and the equipment, supplies, and facilities they will need before you can develop a budget. This is simply the logical sequence of events. Understanding where you are going will free you up to think creatively while you are designing the program or service, and it will help you to avoid some common pitfalls during program budget development. They include:

- Focusing on the money first
- Referring to the library's budget
- A deficit mentality
- Irrational thinking
- Negative mind-set of leadership

One major obstacle that gets in the way of providing effective programs and services is focusing first on the money. When you are working on a program budget, it is a natural response to want to refer constantly to the library's budget. Don't get confused by referring to the library's budget at this point. The library's budget is not your North Star. Instead, the program or service's goals and the objectives you want to accomplish should guide you. Think about the difference your program or service will make for people, rather than your inability to pay for it. There are ways to find resources that are not in the library's budget.

Some librarians are of the mind-set that their libraries are poor and lacking in resources. These librarians may use the library's inadequate resources as an excuse for doing nothing. Not only does this deficit mentality get in the way of providing effective programs and services; unfortunately, it can also become a pattern that over time obstructs any change or innovative thinking in a library. Soon, the library stagnates. Stagnant libraries are not going to survive.

No one can know that the library can't implement a new program or service before it has even been discussed, considered, or planned. Imagine you would like to build a new house, but before you even think about what it might look like, you decide you can't afford it—or someone else tells you that you can't afford it. Then you do nothing. How do you know you can't afford it? Afford what? You haven't even made a plan so you don't even know what "it" is. This is irrational thinking. You cannot conclude that you can't afford to do something when you don't even know what it is.

Most libraries are financially challenged these days. This is no surprise to librarians. Yet, some librarians with the smallest budgets are planning and implementing new and innovative programs and services to effectively meet their community's changing needs. Others are mired in the past, providing the same old worn-out programs with no awareness of their community's current needs, convinced they can do nothing because they have no money. What separates these two approaches? Primarily, it is the mind-set of the leadership. Leaders of "stuck" libraries allow the thought of limited dollars and small budgets to obstruct their ability to act. Unfortunately, they also obstruct the creative ideas of the librarians they manage. Everyone loses.

Libraries need fearless leaders who are willing to find the necessary resources to provide programs and services their communities need. Everything you need to implement an effective program or service doesn't have to be in the form of money already in the library's budget. Once you know what you need, you can gather the resources by forming partnerships and collaborating, seeking alternative funding, "hiring" volunteers, or targeting specific in-kind donations from local businesses, for instance. In her article "Something from Nothing—A Library for a Nontraditional School," Lisa Johnson (2014) describes how to create effective library programs and services in a nontraditional school by seeking partnerships, being innovative with spaces, accepting donations, and being creative when you search for funding. The possibilities are endless once you know what you plan to do and the resources you need to do it.

⑥ Creating the Personnel Budget

At this stage, you have what you need to create a personnel budget for your program or service. To do this, you must reconfigure the information you have already compiled in your activities list and time line in the previous chapter. List each position, all of the activities each one will perform, and the number of hours required for each task. Add together all of the hours required of each position. For budgetary purposes, use a one-year time frame if the program is ongoing. Table 9.1 on the next page contains an example of personnel activities and hours for the makerspace program in the previous chapter.

Next, determine what each position is paid. If staff members in the positions will be working on the program or providing the service, use their current salaries. If you have a consultant position, find out the going rate for a similar consulting position. If you have the opportunity to use a temporary employee pool for a position, research the cost of a temporary employee qualified to do the expected duties. Determine the hourly pay by dividing the yearly salary by fifty-two weeks to find the weekly salary, and then divide that amount by forty hours to determine the hourly pay. Then multiply the hourly pay by the number of hours they will work on the project. For full-time employees, add the cost of benefits, usually around 30 percent of the salary. For consultant positions, add taxes, if applicable. If library staff expects a raise during the time frame of the program or service, include the raise in the personnel budget. To determine the cost of benefits, consult with the personnel department or human resources officer. These costs can fluctuate, and you want to ensure that you are covering the cost for a project that will be implemented in the future.

When you have completed this step for all positions, add together the total amounts. Now you have a personnel budget for your program or service that includes individual pay and total program personnel costs. For an example, see table 9.2 on page 103. You must include all personnel costs associated with a program or service in the personnel budget. Never leave out a required activity or necessary hours because "the staff member does that anyway" or because "it is already part of their regular job." When you are planning a new program, the staff member is not already doing anything to contribute to it because it does not yet exist. Folding new activities into someone's job without acknowledging that they will take time or associated costs is irresponsible—and it is poor management.

If you work in a library where library staff members are required to absorb extra duties to implement a new program on top of their existing duties, they probably resist the idea of new programs and services. This only makes sense. When people have to do more work without recognition, this eventually leads to resentment. Staff members run the other way when someone mentions a new program or service. In their experience, implementing something new only means they have more work to do in the same number of hours they already work for the same pay. Unfortunately, this practice is not uncommon. It is a sign that leadership is not in touch with their employees' actual duties and how

Table 9.1. Personnel Activities and Hours Example

Technology Librarian	Hours
Investigate, select, and request order for 3-D printer and software	15
Investigate, select, and request order for furniture	15
Learn how to use software and 3-D printer	10
Create policies, guidelines for makerspace, computers, and 3-D printer use	20
Evaluate program	40
Manage program	105
Total	205

Instruction Librarian	Hours
Learn how to use software and 3-D printer	10
Design classes to teach using software and 3-D printer	80
Provide training on how to use software and 3-D printer for library staff	20
Prepare instructional materials	40
Teach classes on how to use software and 3-D printer	50
Total	200

Computer Technician	Hours
Assess capability of current computers to run hardware and software	10
Assist with software and 3-D printer selection	5
Upgrade computers to handle the software and 3-D printer	10
Set up 3-D printer	10
Install software	10
Provide ongoing support on software and 3-D printer use	105
Total	150

Administrative Assistant	Hours
Purchase 3-D printer, software, and furniture	5
Purchase necessary upgrades for computers	5
Schedule makerspace for teaching classes	10
Advertise classes	40
Total	60

Table 9.2. Personnel Budget Example

POSITION	PROGRAM SALARY	BENEFITS	TOTAL
Technology Librarian 205 hours @ $33.65/hour	$6,898.25	$2,069.48	$8,967.73
Instruction Librarian 200 hours @ $31.25/hour	$6,250.00	$1,875.00	$8,125.00
Computer Technician 150 hours @ $17.32/hour	$2,598.00	$779.40	$3,377.40
Administrative Assistant 60 hours @ $12.67/hour	$760.20	$228.06	$988.26
Total Program Personnel Cost	**$16,506.45**	**$4,951.94**	**$21,458.39**

long it takes to do them. No one is paying attention by removing, decreasing, or shifting their current duties to make time for them to do the new ones. When this happens, an unspoken message is communicated that management thinks staff members have extra time when they are not doing any work, or they can easily add more tasks similar to the ones they are already doing. This devalues staff, and employee morale suffers.

Most people agree to a clause in their position description that states they are responsible for "other duties as required"; however, in most cases this does not mean that management can continue to pile on more work without compensation. It is leadership's responsibility to coordinate work assignments so it is realistic to perform them within the number of hours worked. If a librarian is paid to work forty hours a week, he should be assigned a weekly workload he can reasonably complete within forty hours. When he is required to perform new duties or activities to implement a new program or service, some of his current duties must be reduced or eliminated, or shifted to another staff member. A full-time employee who is working at 100 percent capacity performing duties that cannot be reduced or shifted to another worker is not a good candidate for working on a new program or service.

Creating the Non-Personnel Budget

Begin to investigate the non-personnel costs of your program or service by making a list of the equipment and supplies you will need to implement it. First, look at your program's goals and objectives, and list what you will need to accomplish what you have planned. Then refer to the activities list for your program and consider which staff members will need to accomplish the program or service activities they will be performing. Does the program or service need a separate dedicated space? What will the overhead cost share be? For budgetary purposes, you need projected costs for all items. Use a one-year time frame covering your fiscal year if the program is ongoing. For example, the makerspace example from the previous chapter might need the following:

Furnishings and Equipment

- 3-D printer and filament
- Furniture for printer, instruction, and additional workspace
- Software for 3-D printer
- Software for upgrading computers

Administrative Expenses

- Printing marketing materials
- Office supplies

Facilities Expenses

- Renovating and reconfiguring space
- Overhead for space, utilities, maintenance, Internet, telephone

Estimate all costs and create a non-personnel budget using the example in table 9.3 as a guide. Subtract any revenue you expect. In the example, the library will charge customers for 3-D printer filament to recover those costs. Then combine the personnel and non-personnel budgets to create one cohesive program budget. The example in table 9.4 on page 106 shows a program budget that combines the personnel budget shown in table 9.2 and the non-personnel budget shown in table 9.3.

Table 9.3. Non-Personnel Budget Example

ITEM	COST	TOTAL
Furnishings and Equipment		
Equipment and Supplies 3-D printer Filament	$2,000 300	$2,300
Furniture (1) Rolling utility cart with locked cabinet for printer and supplies (1) Table for instruction (1) Whiteboard easel for instruction (2) Adjustable computer workstations @ $540 each	$509 630 220 540	$1,899
Software 3-D printer software (3) Windows 8 upgrade @ $200 each	$300 600	$900
Furnishings and Equipment Total		**$5,099**
Administrative Expenses		
Printing flyers, brochures Office supplies	$300 150	$450
Administrative Expenses Total		**$450**
Facilities		
Renovating and reconfiguring space Overhead share includes space, utilities, maintenance, Internet, telephone	$2,000 1,700	$2,000 1,700
Facilities Total		**$3,700**
Total Non-Personnel Program Costs		$9,249
Revenue Filament sales		-$300
Balance Non-Personnel Program Costs		$8,949

⟳ Understanding Program Budgets vs. Line Item Budgets

A budget such as the example in table 9.4 on page 106, developed for a specific program or service, is called a program budget. Some organizations operate using program budgets, which categorize expenses by programs, services, activities, or products. Program budgets are organized around outputs, or how the library is meeting needs. In a program budget, each program appears separately with its own subset of line-item costs. In the case of libraries, program budgets may be grouped by categories such as teen programs, adult programs, and children's programs. Program costs are summed for each individual program, supplying total costs for every program and service. A total cost for each category is helpful for reporting and budget management purposes. This makes it easier to compare program costs and to analyze the types of costs within and across programs.

Line-Item Budgets

The line-item budget is probably the most common budgeting method used in libraries today. Line-item budgets are input-centered. They arrange costs by input or type of good purchased library-wide such as supplies, equipment, facilities, salaries, technology, and books. Table 9.5 on page 107 shows how you might arrange a line-item budget.

With line-item budgets, it is easy to generate reports about expenditures from year to year, or determine how much money is left for the library to spend on each type of good. Municipalities, universities, and school districts often require all departments to use a line-item format for consistency across departments, easy budget comparisons, making projections, and tracking expenditures. One disadvantage of line-item budgets is that they do not clearly reflect the cost of individual programs and services. Program and service costs are spread across the budget and are fragmented, hidden somewhere within types of goods. This means that when librarians must make budget cuts, they often make cuts across the board or by goods or line items rather than by streamlining less effective programs and services. Line-item budgets invite decisions such as cutting back 20 percent on book purchases or closing ten branches. "Many libraries in this country . . . have been constrained by the type of information that their line-item budgets generate, which, in turn, constrains them to think in terms of line items rather than programmatically" (Robinson and Robinson 1994).

Program Budgets

Libraries operate from strategic plans that are organized by goals, objectives, and activities. The result is the delivery of programs and services that meet community needs—or outputs. Because program budgets are output-centered, common sense tells us that program budgets are probably more library-friendly than line-item budgets. It is difficult to be guided by the library's mission when you are working with types of goods purchased without reference to what librarians are doing with the goods to benefit the community. You can easily lose track of the library's purpose when you are working with a line-item budget. Conversely, program budgets are built around what the library is doing to benefit the community.

It is essential to know what the library's programs and services cost. Knowing this information gives librarians the power to justify costs, add new programs and services, or strategically shift funds between programs when necessary. We are in a time of economic hardship and significant change for libraries and communities. In most libraries, dollars must be reallocated in the face of shrinking budgets and increasing needs. Directors must

Table 9.4. Program Budget Example

PERSONNEL			
POSITION	**PROGRAM SALARY**	**BENEFITS**	**TOTAL**
Technology Librarian 205 hours @ $33.65/hour	$6,898.25	$2,069.48	$8,967.73
Instruction Librarian 200 hours @ $31.25/hour	$6,250.00	$1,875.00	$8,125.00
Computer Technician 150 hours @ $17.32/hour	$2,598.00	$779.40	$3,377.40
Administrative Assistant 60 hours @ $12.67/hour	$760.20	$228.06	$988.26
Total Program Personnel Cost	**$16,506.45**	**$4,951.94**	**$21,458.39**

NON-PERSONNEL		
ITEM	**COST**	**TOTAL**
Furnishings and Equipment		
Equipment and Supplies 3-D printer Filament	$2,000 300	$2,300
Furniture (1) Rolling utility cart with locked cabinet for printer and supplies (1) Table for instruction (1) Whiteboard easel for instruction (2) Adjustable computer workstations @ $540 each	$509 630 220 540	$1,899
Software 3-D printer software (3) Windows 8 upgrade @ $200 each	$300 600	$900
Furnishings and Equipment Total		**$5,099**
Administrative Expenses		
Printing flyers, brochures Office supplies	$300 150	$450
Administrative Expenses Total		**$450**
Facilities		
Renovating and reconfiguring space Overhead share includes space, utilities, maintenance, Internet, telephone	$2,000 1,700	$2,000 1,700
Facilities Total		**$3,700**
Subtotal Non-Personnel Program Costs		**$9,249**
Revenue Filament sales		-$300
Total Non-Personnel Program Costs		**$8,949**
Total Program Personnel Cost		**+21,458.39**
TOTAL PROGRAM COST		**$30,407.39**

Table 9.5. Line-Item Budget Example

OPERATING EXPENDITURES	AMOUNT
Salaries and wages	$25,650
Employee benefits	16,350
Books	7,035
Periodicals	1,470
Video materials	1,050
Audio materials	420
Software and databases	525
Contracted services	1,050
Continuing education	1,050
Programs	525
Telecommunications	1,575
Utilities	4,200
Equipment repair	525
Supplies	1,575
Operating Expenditures Total	**$63,000**
CAPITAL EXPENDITURES	AMOUNT
Equipment replacement	2,000
New shelving	1,000
Capital Expenditures Total	**$3,000**
Total of All Expenditures	**$66,000**

know what part of the total budget is being allocated to each program or service to know where to make adjustments and wisely use resources.

In October 2013 Rahm Emanuel, mayor of Chicago, stated, "Budgets are statements of values and priorities" as he increased funding for the Chicago Public Library's YOUmedia digital skills program by $500,000 (Petersen 2013). It was the program he funded, not separate line items for program equipment, supplies, and personnel. Program budgets can be powerful tools for demonstrating the value of a program that is meeting real needs. It is likely that the need for funding this successful program attracted Mr. Emanuel's attention rather than a general desire on his part to increase line items in the library's budget.

Program Budget or Line Item Budget?

Even if your library's budget is in the line-item format, you must develop program budgets when you are planning individual programs and services. Your larger organization may still require a line-item format for the library's overall budget; however, if at all possible, convert the library's working budget to a program budget. Program budgets can be time-consuming to prepare, and you may need to translate the program budget back into a line-item format for reporting purposes; however, it is well worth the time. Working with a budget that supports the library's goals, objectives, and outcomes instills confidence in what librarians are doing and fosters a more positive outlook for the future. Knowing what each program costs and the detailed budget for each program and service provides more latitude when adjusting program activities and shifting or reallocating costs across programs and services.

Program budgets facilitate the ability to change. Over time, working with a budget that reflects the programs and services librarians are providing to benefit the community will reinforce the mission and purpose of the library. When the needs of a community shift, it is a much easier and more logical task to determine next steps when you are working with a program budget. Resources can be shifted from programs that are designed to meet needs that are no longer present to new programs that meet emerging needs.

This detailed knowledge about program costs and resources also gives you the power to advocate meaningfully for the library's programs and services. You can speak to potential partners with confidence about the effectiveness of programs and the resources you need. You also have the ability to target appropriate alternative funding sources if necessary.

Key Points

One of the most important aspects of planning programs and services is allocating adequate resources. Resources are the people, equipment, supplies, materials, and space your program requires. When you develop a budget for your program or service, you gain a clear understanding of what resources are necessary for implementation.

- One major obstacle to providing effective programs and services is focusing first on the money.
- Libraries need fearless leaders who are willing to find the necessary resources to provide programs and services their communities need.
- When librarians are open-minded and creative, effective programs and services can be implemented in libraries that have very limited resources.
- You must include in the personnel budget all personnel costs associated with a program or service. Never leave out a required activity or necessary hours because "the staff member does that anyway" or because "it is already part of their regular job."
- Even if your library's budget is in the line-item format, you must develop program budgets when you are planning new programs and services.
- Program budgets facilitate the ability to change and give you the power to advocate meaningfully for the library's programs and services.

The next chapter will explore how to identify funding opportunities to help you implement effective programs and services.

References

Johnson, Lisa. 2014. "Something from Nothing—A Library for a Nontraditional School." *School Library Monthly* 30, no. 6 (March): 36–38.

Petersen, Karyn. 2013. "Chicago Public Library to Expand YOUmedia Program in 2014," October. http://www.slj.com/2013/10/budgets-funding/chicago-public-library-to-expand-you media-program-in-2014/#_.

Robinson, Barbara M., and Sherman Robinson. 1994. "Strategic Planning and Program Budgeting for Libraries." *Library Trends* 42, no. 3 (Winter): 420–47.

Funding Effective Programs and Services

NOW YOU HAVE A PLAN FOR YOUR PROGRAM OR SERVICE IDEA that includes a goal and objectives, outcomes, activities, personnel, a time line, and a budget. Depending on the nature of your workplace, a procedure for proposing new program or service ideas will be recommended. You may have informally mentioned your idea to your director who was initially receptive. He or she may have asked you to create a plan including personnel required, a time line, and budget. Once you have everything in place, this may be the right time to submit your proposal for permission to proceed.

If you work in a large academic library or organization, the process may be more formal; committees may submit proposals for new programs and services to an administrator at specific times during the year. Regardless of your situation, your plan or proposal will include a budget. You may be confident the library's budget contains enough money to cover the cost of your proposed program or service; however, it is always wise to have alternative funding suggestions in mind or ready to submit along with your plan or proposal. Do not assume that the administration knows you are prepared to find funding for your project. Be clear that you have thought about the funding and that you have ideas about securing funding that may be required to implement your program or service. You don't want to be turned away at this late date because "the library can't afford it." Be prepared with a solid answer and ready to go into action should you be met with this tired phrase.

⦿ Understanding Different Funding Options

Regardless of your situation, think about the likely response of the person who will be considering your suggestion or proposal. Will the cost be important to him? Will he scrutinize the program budget? Is he likely to say the library has enough money? Or will he say the library's budget does not include enough money to fund the program? Will he say maybe next year, or never? Will he give you the opportunity to find the money to support your program if you have ideas about where to find it? Sadly, many librarians walk away, defeated, when met with these hard questions. Don't let this be you.

You have devoted a great deal of time and energy to planning a new program or service, and you want to do everything in your power to see it implemented. Here are some things you can do:

- Understand your library's financial environment and the mind-set of the person holding the purse strings.
- Educate yourself about your library's budget and how it is organized.
- Talk to the director or finance officer about where money may be found to fund your program or service idea.
- Talk to board members responsible for making funding decisions.
- Make a presentation to the board or financial officer/committee explaining the program and how it will benefit the community.
- Anticipate possible objections and be prepared with suggestions about alternative ways to fund your program or service.
- Break down your program or service into sections or parts that can be implemented— and funded—in phases.
- Be prepared to work hard to secure funding for a new program or service.
- Don't be discouraged. Sometimes it takes more than one try to get your point across.

If a program or service is necessary, yet your budget is inadequate, you are obligated to explore alternative ways to implement it. Librarians are responsible for meeting the community's information needs, not for cutting programs and services to match the shrinking budget. Even in difficult economic times, librarians can be proactive on behalf of their communities. Don't lose sight of what you are doing. Focus on the people, not on the money. When the budget has been cut, the needs don't disappear. Find a way to fund the programs and services that will make the most difference in your community. You can approach funding challenges multiple ways, including finding money in the library's existing budget, forming partnerships, working with the library's friends' group or foundation, and seeking grants.

⑥ Finding Money in the Library's Budget

The preferred way to fund a new library program or service is to use money that is already in the library's budget. When you manage the library's finances actively and continuously to ensure that the money in the budget is efficiently funding the highest priorities and meeting the greatest needs, this is possible. By monitoring the effectiveness of programs and services, you will know where to shift money from less effective programs and services to more effective ones. When you continuously evaluate all programs and services, you are able to pinpoint areas for improving or streamlining activities, selecting the right products, or using the staff's time more wisely and thereby expending funds more efficiently.

This is a sensitive approach if you are in a library where the budget is protected for the purposes of providing the same ongoing programs year in and year out. First ask if everything library staff is doing now is meeting the community's current needs. Are all library programs and services effective and efficient? Are they helping to meet the library's goals and objectives? Are evaluations telling you that all programs and services are accomplishing their objectives? If the answer to any of these questions is no, or if no one knows the answers, some funding in the budget probably can be shifted to implement a new effective program or service. Somewhere in a library's existing budget is enough money to fund at least partially a vital new program or service that will make a difference in people's lives.

Librarians must look more closely at how they are spending the library's money and, if necessary, cut back on or eliminate ineffective programs and services. This is not only a librarian's job, but it is essential for the survival of libraries. At one time librarians could rely on continued funding and a steady revenue stream. The money was there, and "everyone loves libraries." This is no longer a viable way to ensure adequate library funding.

Today, librarians must demonstrate the effectiveness of library programs and services with hard data and trusted evaluation methodologies. If you are measuring your library's success by program attendance or how many reference questions are asked, these are not indicators of effectiveness or success. Accepted evaluation methodologies can help you determine where money in the budget can be used to implement new programs and services (see chapter 12).

The Challenge of Line-Item Budgets Again

As covered in chapter 9, most librarians work with line-item budgets. They do not reflect the programs and services librarians provide; instead, they represent categories of things purchased such as supplies, equipment, subscriptions, materials, and salaries. This format does not reveal how the things purchased translate into programs and services; therefore, it is very difficult to shift money from one program to another. This may be why some librarians think about the money in the budget in terms of the things they need to purchase rather than funding programs and services that the community needs. When you see the library's funding from the perspective of what the library needs in a climate of shrinking budgets, it is very difficult to entertain the possibility of new programs and services. When all the money in the budget is allocated for purchasing the things the library needs, and the amount of money decreases every year, the chance of implementing new programs seems slimmer.

This is an ever-shrinking paradigm. When staff members perceive that money is unavailable in the library's budget for new endeavors, eventually they stop putting any effort into developing innovative ideas for new programs and services. Staff members blindly provide what they have always provided in the past. The same community members come to the library for the same programs they have attended for decades. People who want new effective services to meet their needs eventually go elsewhere.

Line-item budgets are not organized in a way that invites change. Many library directors or finance officers routinely set aside blocks of money to buy the things that fund the same programs and services the library has provided in the past. Some do this out of habit, because it is the path of least resistance, or because they are required by their larger organizations to keep line-item budgets for reporting purposes. Some don't know how to re-create the budget into a more useful tool. After all, a librarian's professional education is focused on information management, not on financial management.

Even visually, line-item budgets look inflexible. Sometimes funds allocated to line items become difficult to change due to a library director's inability to see beyond them to the programs and services that they fund. Thus, when approached about new programs or services, these directors say this money is not available because it is already committed to routine library operations or other programs and services. They cannot see how this view of the budget has paralyzed them and the library, disabled library staff, and deprived the community of needed programs and services.

If you are committed to implementing an effective program or service, yet you are told no funding is available for it, you must generate ideas about how to fund your program with money or efforts from outside the library's budget. In some cases, you will need to secure or raise the funds yourself. You may need to explain this new paradigm of focusing on the community's needs to the library director or board members. Librarians who are focused on the library rather than on the community are headed down a dead end.

Forming Partnerships

Providing effective programs and services does not necessarily require finding all of the funding in the library's budget. A partnership is a relationship created through a commitment between two or more entities that join together, combining their assets and resources to reach a common goal. Partnerships between libraries and other community agencies, libraries, or businesses work best when they have a goal that can be better achieved together than apart. Everyone benefits from partnerships, but ultimately the community benefits the most.

Partnerships extend the capacity of librarians and others to provide effective programs and services to meet community needs. When you partner with others who have common goals and aim to meet similar community needs, your chances of implementing a successful program or service increase. A partner may be able to offer a resource you lack, or you may be able to offer what the partner lacks to implement a program. Good partners for libraries include:

- Other libraries (public, school, special, academic)
- Community organizations (youth, senior, arts and culture, ethnic, and service organizations)
- Literacy organizations

- Public and private schools
- Colleges and universities
- Businesses (grocery, banks, bookstores, retail)
- Public agencies/departments (parks and recreation, cultural departments, public health, transportation, education)
- Utility companies (power, gas, cable, phone)
- Media (print, radio, TV)
- Community events (fairs, festivals, art tours, etc.)

The right partner for your program or service:

- Has program and/or service goals and objectives similar to yours
- Serves your program or service's target population
- Meets the same needs that your program or service aims to meet
- Has the resources that will help achieve success

Knowing what you lack to implement the program will help you know where to look for partners. Be specific about what you need and whom you approach. Partners can provide many kinds of resources, for example:

- Materials
- Expertise
- Equipment
- Volunteers
- Public relations
- Marketing
- Printing services
- Space
- Technology
- Teachers or instructors

Do your research and be selective. Do not randomly cold call potential partners without a program or service design or plan. Make sure you are cleared by your administration to contact potential partners. Be prepared to tell potential partners what you need to implement your program as well as what the library is providing. Do not waste their time with vague ideas and half-baked plans. When you contact community partner prospects, you are representing the library. Do a thorough job to prepare before contacting anyone about being a partner. Successful partnerships:

- Address common goals and objectives of the partners
- Maximize benefits to the community
- Incorporate sustainability
- Require constant communication and evaluation

Partnerships are not about ways to benefit the library. They are not for the purpose of marketing the library or outreach. This is very shortsighted. Remember, the reason for offering library programs and services is to make a difference in your community by meeting their needs. Partnerships are about working with others and sharing resources to help make a difference for people. If your goal is to increase gate counts, circulation, and program attendance to make better numbers for your annual report, you are misguided. Approaching partnerships with the purpose of gaining something for the library will not end well.

Collaboration

The meaning of partnerships versus collaborations is often confused. Collaboration is a process that engages diverse entities to come together to find solutions to problems. Collaborators are likely involved from the planning stages on, finding the best way to address a need, followed by participation in designing a service or program to meet the need. In collaboration, each entity operates independently and maintains control over its own resources. When you collaborate, you work on solutions together with people from other organizations who may have different views of the same problem. Some collaborators may also become partners. Partners combine resources for the purpose of implementing a program or project. This may happen when a collaborator offers a resource that is necessary to implement the project. Collaborators make great partners because they have been involved with a program or service since its conception and they have an interest in its success. They already have buy-in and ownership of the program.

ⓖ Working with Library Friends' Groups and Library Foundations

Many libraries have Friends of the Library groups whose purpose is to raise funds and advocate for the library. Friends don't act independently or decide on their own which programs and services they will fund. Ideally, the friends are represented on the planning team, thus they are acutely aware of the library's goals and objectives, plans and priorities. The friends and the library must be in alignment. Friends do not decide what programs and services the library will offer based on their own judgment or the wishes of a generous benefactor. The library's plan dictates what funds are needed and their purpose. It is up to the library director to communicate regularly with friends' groups, informing them about the community's needs, the library's plans and priorities, and new programs and services librarians have proposed. The director tells the friends what funds the library needs. Friends then raise funds specifically for what the library has planned. If members of the friends' group disagree with the library's plans, then consider inviting them to the next planning session where their input will be considered.

Let the friends know about programs and services the library is planning and what funds are needed to implement them. Be specific, telling them what the money they raise will purchase and how it will benefit the community. This allows the friends to advocate for what you are doing while they are raising the funds. People are much more likely to donate money when they know what it is for and how people will benefit. As the friends talk about your plans in the community, they will gain ownership of the programs and services, and they will likely have more interest in what you are doing now and in the future.

Ambitious friends' groups have been known to present ideas for launching large-scale capital campaigns on their own without first consulting the library director or referring to the library's plans (Radford 2011). It is not up to the friends to determine how the library will meet community needs. Allowing this to happen is not only a recipe for disaster, but it derails the capacity of the friends to raise money for what the library needs to implement programs and services in the future. Directors must be strong leaders when it comes to the friends' fund-raising efforts. It is a big waste of everyone's time and money to launch capital campaigns for things that are not in the library's plan.

Use your friends' group wisely. Friends can help acquire significant funds the library needs to provide programs and services. They do not just volunteer at library events, hold bake sales, and host author events. The friends' leadership must have a highly developed capacity to raise funds, and they must be focused on the library's priorities. It is the library director's job to focus their energy and use them efficiently. Avoid a "hands-off" approach where the friends raise funds aimlessly for generic ongoing programs. It is difficult to keep talented people with sharp fund-raising skills as members or officers when they are not given any direction or they don't feel as if they are making a difference.

Many libraries have formed library foundations that involve community members who are not library users as well as library patrons to advocate for the library and raise funds. Library foundations are 501(c)(3) nonprofits, allowing for more grant opportunities and offering donors tax deductions on their contributions. Friends' groups can also be 501(c)(3) nonprofits with the same benefits, and they may involve nonusers as well. Librarians have found that people have more confidence in foundations, they attract more powerful leaders, help create more partnerships, and carry more clout when it comes to fund-raising. Whether a friends' group or a foundation is more appropriate for your library, a group or entity devoted to raising funds is necessary.

◎ Seeking Grants

Some librarians are not interested in seeking alternative funding such as grants because they think that grants only mean more work. This thinking is not accurate. It impedes librarians' ability to attract funding for new and innovative programs and services, and it sometimes robs communities of effective programs and services. When librarians are willing to cut programs and services rather than seek grant funding to keep them going in hard times, libraries are in trouble. As a profession, librarians must work to change this by building grant work into their jobs. Myriad resources explore grants for libraries and nonprofits, including how to find grant opportunities and write proposals. Once you have done the groundwork, grant work is not all that difficult. The basic steps in the grant process are:

1. Making the commitment and understanding the process
2. Planning for success
3. Discovering and designing the program or service
4. Organizing the grant team
5. Understanding the sources and resources
6. Researching and selecting the right grant
7. Creating and submitting the winning proposal
8. Getting funded and implementing the project
9. Reviewing and continuing the process (MacKellar and Gerding)

Because you have already planned, discovered, and designed your program or service, you now need to learn enough about the grant process so you understand it, and then commit to it. If you are in a larger public or school library system or part of an academic institution, you will likely form a grant team to share the work. In small libraries, you and another person may be all you need on your team; however, make sure to include your partners and representatives from the community. For small projects that will require short proposals or minimal outside funding, a large team is not necessary; however, don't attempt to do all the work yourself. Grant work is not a one-person job.

Understanding the Sources and Resources

Take time to learn about the sources—or where grants come from—and the resources available for researching grants. This knowledge will save you lots of time in your research. Grants are awarded from two primary sources: private and government. Private grants are awarded by foundations and nonprofits; corporations and corporate foundations; clubs and organizations; and professional and trade associations. Government grants come from the federal government, state government, or local government (i.e., county, parish, municipality, city, town, or village).

Directories and Databases

You can find both private and government grant opportunities in print and online directories and databases. Some of the most comprehensive directories of foundations that fund programs and services are published by the Foundation Center in print and online. For example:

- Foundation Directory Online (https://fdo.foundationcenter.org/)
- *The Foundation Directories*. The Foundation Center, New York.
- *National Directory of Corporate Giving*. The Foundation Center, New York.

In addition, the *Annual Register of Grant Support*, published by Information Today, Medford, New Jersey, is a comprehensive guide to more than three thousand grant-giving organizations.

Certain grant directories and databases compile grant opportunities in a specific topic or subject area, gender, or age group. The Foundation Center publishes the following digital grant guides that list foundation grant opportunities by the purpose of the program or service you want to fund:

- Arts, culture, and the humanities
- Capacity building, management, and technical assistance
- Community and economic development
- Elementary and secondary education
- Environmental protection and animal welfare
- Foreign and international programs
- Higher education
- Hospitals and health organizations
- Mental health, addiction, and crisis services
- People with disabilities
- Religion, religious welfare, and religious education
- Services for the homeless

These Foundation Center grant guides list grant opportunities by age range or gender of target population served:

- Aging
- Children and youth
- Women and girls

Some directories list funders located in most states and some regions in the United States. The Foundation Center maintains a bibliography listing them at http://foundationcenter.org/getstarted/topical/sl_dir.html. These directories list smaller funders that may not appear in the large directories, and some list funders outside the state or area that fund programs within the geographic area. Investigate community foundations in your region. The staff at your local community foundation should be aware of current funding opportunities in your area and can guide you in the right direction. A staff member may be willing to meet with you to discuss the program or service you need funded. Depending on their services, they may contact you or send you notifications of potential funding as it becomes available.

Federal Grants

The federal government is the largest source of grant funding in the United States. Grants.gov (www.grants.gov) is the central clearinghouse for all of the discretionary grants offered by the twenty-six federal grant-making agencies. Available grants are arranged by category, agency, and eligibility, and searchable by keyword. Alternatively, you can visit websites of the individual agencies that are likely to offer a grant for a project like yours. For example, some library programs and services might be funded by grants from the following:

- Institute of Museum and Library Services (www.imls.gov)
- National Endowment for the Arts (www.arts.gov)
- National Endowment for the Humanities (www.neh.gov)
- National Historical Publications and Records Commission (www.archives.gov/nhprc)
- National Network of Libraries of Medicine (www.nnlm.gov)
- U.S. Department of Education (www.ed.gov)

Grants for Libraries

Resources for grants that fund libraries and information science projects might be appropriate for your research, depending on the purpose of your program or service. These include:

- Library Grants Blog (http://librarygrants.blogspot.com/)
- *ALA Book of Library Grant Money*. Chicago. American Library Association.

Do not limit your research to directories or databases that list only grants for libraries. Most private and government funders award grants to fund programs because they will make a difference for people in a specific area or discipline, age range, or gender that matches their interests or priorities. In general, funders don't fund programs only offered by a particular kind of institution such as a library. Focus on the purpose of your program or service. Then research funders that fund programs and services that have the same purpose as yours.

Your state library agency receives Library Services and Technology Act (LSTA) funding from the Institute of Museum and Library Services (IMLS). This is the only federal funding exclusively for libraries. To distribute this funding to libraries throughout your state based on its priorities, a state library may conduct competitive grant competitions. Check with your state library about available LSTA funding and how to apply for it.

State and Local Agencies and Departments

Investigate your state, county, or city agencies, or departments such as arts councils and humanities councils, historical societies, and departments of education for grant opportunities that match the purpose of your program or service.

Clubs and Organizations

Local funding opportunities available through clubs and organizations are usually not widely advertised. Network with involved friends and community members to stay abreast of available funding for programs like yours. Speak at local clubs and organizations about the programs and services you would like to implement, how the community will benefit, and the funding or other help you need make them a reality.

Researching and Selecting the Right Grant

Before beginning your research, make a list of keywords that describe your program or service. The keywords will help you select the right resources to use and formulate specific searches. Avoid using the words "library," "libraries," or "library projects" as keywords. As a librarian, you know to begin your research broadly. Shift your focus from the library to what the project is about. Allow the need your program or service will meet in the community to guide you as you make your list. Who are the people the program or service will serve? What is their age group? How will their lives improve as a result of your program or service? What discipline does your program or service encompass?

Remember that grants are about funding what the community needs, not about funding what the library needs. Below are some programs that illustrate lists of keywords as examples:

Community Garden Program

Many libraries are pioneering programs in response to their communities' interest in gardening and growing their own food. High Point Public Library's (NC) Teaching Garden teaches people to grow and cultivate their own food. The program offers cooking classes and gardening classes, and donates produce to less fortunate members of the community. Keywords might be:

- Gardening
- Seeds

- Horticulture
- Community gardens
- Vegetables
- Food production
- Self-sustaining
- Cooking
- Food donation
- Children
- Teens
- Adults

Community Digital Content Program

Library YOU at Escondido (California) Public Library focuses on collecting and sharing local knowledge through videos and podcasts. The project encourages community members to create digital content at the library by providing training on technology, and making videos and podcasts available to the community. Keywords to consider are:

- Technology training
- Podcasts
- Videos
- Local history
- Recording
- Digital content
- Teens
- Adults

Creative Aging Programs

These programs, implemented in public libraries throughout New York State, support collaborations between professional teaching artists and public libraries through the implementation of free instructional arts programs for older adults. Possible keywords include:

- Arts
- Creativity
- Older adults
- Mature adults
- Aging
- Elderly
- Crafts

Use the keyword list to perform subject searches in online directories or to navigate your way through the large print directories that are usually arranged by subject area or indexed by subject. Keywords will also help you discover the appropriate resources for finding a funding opportunity in the topic area, or target age group or gender your program will serve.

Competing for Funding

It is unrealistic to think that money will to continue to flow to your library with minimal effort. Relying on the notion that people love libraries so the money will follow is not a solid fund-raising strategy. As the money gets tighter, the competition for dollars becomes stiffer. In municipalities, the limited funds are going to the departments that can demonstrate their worth. Residents are thinking twice before voting in favor of yet another library bond issue that will increase their property taxes. If you are not actively focused on the purpose of the library and how librarians make a difference by meeting people's information needs, promoting lifelong learning, supporting research and scholarship, improving literacy, encouraging reading, teaching technology skills, or otherwise improving the quality of life for people, the funding will eventually disappear. You must be committed to the importance of your programs and services to be able to compete for funding successfully.

Revisit the community profile you developed and community needs you discovered in chapters 2 and 3. Recall the process of designing the program or service to meet those specific needs. Remember the purpose of your project, its goal, or what it will accomplish. Clarify the objectives in your own mind and how accomplishing them will make a difference for people. This will refresh your enthusiasm for your program and help you build a logical case for its importance. When your program or service makes sense to you, and you can demonstrate its potential value, you will be able promote it passionately. Talk in the community about your plans, and write proposals to fund new programs and services. Tell your family and friends about the programs and services you are planning. Soon you will begin to attract funding and support from multiple sources.

Focus on what you want to accomplish and how people will benefit, not on what the library is lacking. You will not be very successful at attracting funding by pleading for money because you don't have enough. Being poor or lacking funds is not a compelling reason for funders to give you money. All libraries need money. Most funders want their grants to make a difference for people, not buy stuff for the library.

Use your program and service plans to be specific. Know what you need and target your fund-raising efforts appropriately. Random talk about needing money for generic ongoing library programs is not going to attract sustainable outside funding. Do the hard work of assessing needs. Eliminate programs or services that are not meeting current needs. Librarians who offer the same programs and services of decades ago because "they've always offered them" will not attract the attention or money of those who want to make the most difference.

Sometimes it is possible to amend your original plan or segment it into multiple parts or phases in order to get a program or service off the ground within your financial means. You must have a solid plan or program design before you investigate these different funding options. Be ready to apply for a grant or accept a donation to fund part of a program.

Changing the Library Funding Model

"Librarians can no longer take their institutions or their support for granted. To succeed or survive in this brave new world, we must stand on our own two feet. The most critical challenge facing librarians as we enter the Third Millennium is how to generate revenue that can replace the institutional support we once assumed would never stop" (Coffman

2000). Building a new funding model for libraries has been a topic in the library science literature for decades, yet libraries still face the same basic funding challenges they have always faced. Why is this?

Change is difficult. Many librarians are accustomed to operating from within a passive model (Zabriskie 2004). Traditionally, patrons came to libraries to get what they needed. Librarians waited for them to arrive and then helped patrons to access and synthesize information, or they disseminated information to those who requested it. To measure their success, librarians counted the numbers of materials circulated and the numbers of people passing through the library doors.

Likewise, when it came to providing programs and services, librarians passively waited to find out how much money was in their budgets before they knew what was possible in the coming year. In hard times they deferred to the more "essential" services such as police, fire, and ambulance for scarce funds. Slowly but surely, library funding shrank, and librarians found themselves in dire straits. To cope, they reduced services and programs. Fewer people came to the library. Working within this passive model waiting for things to change is clearly not the way to success.

Librarians must develop an active model from which to operate, including funding libraries. Active librarians seek to determine the current needs of their communities. They reach out to all community members, library users and nonusers alike. They plan creative and innovative programs and services designed to make a difference in people's lives. They are envelope pushers who advocate for their communities and partner with other libraries, agencies, and organizations to maximize the effectiveness of their efforts to make a difference. It only makes sense for librarians to develop an active funding model to match this new active librarianship model. You cannot be a creative, innovative, out-of-the-box thinker and then sit back to see if enough money will appear in the budget when it is revealed. It is a librarian's job to actively seek funding for effective programs and services, instead of reacting to shrinking budgets by cutting services and programs or rejecting new ideas due to lack of funding.

It is time for librarians to develop new sources of revenue. Other cultural and educational institutions including museums, zoos, orchestras, historical societies, nature centers, public universities, public television, and radio have adopted a plural funding model. They cultivate a variety of revenue sources that include memberships, contributions, sponsorships, and business ventures. These institutions and others no longer depend solely on tax revenue as most public libraries do (Coffman 2006). The time has come for librarians to shift to a new funding model.

Key Points

Even if you are confident enough money is in the library's budget to cover the costs of your program or service, it is always wise to have alternative funding suggestions in mind or ready to submit along with your plan or proposal. In this chapter, you learned about multiple ways to approach funding challenges, including finding money in the library's existing budget, forming partnerships, working with the library's friends' group or foundation, and seeking grants.

- Have alternative funding suggestions ready to submit to your director along with your program plan or proposal.

- Focus on the people, not on the money.
- The preferred way to fund a new library program or service is to use money that is already in the library's budget.
- Partnerships extend the capacity of librarians and others to provide effective programs and services to meet community needs.
- Knowing what you lack to implement the program will help you know where to look for partners. Be specific about what you need and whom you approach.
- The director tells the Friends of the Library or library foundation what funds the library needs. Friends or foundations then raise funds specifically for what the library has planned.
- Grants are awarded from two primary sources: private and government.
- Once you have done the groundwork, grant work is not all that difficult; however, grant work is not a one-person job.
- Taking the time to learn about the sources and the resources available for researching grants will save you time.
- Relying on the notion that people love libraries so the money will follow is not a solid fund-raising strategy.
- Focus on what you want to accomplish and how people will benefit, not on what the library is lacking.

The next chapter will cover implementing effective library services and programs. Once you have the funding and partnerships in place, you are ready to put your plans into action.

References

Coffman, Steve. 2000. "And Now, a Word from Our Sponsors . . . Alternative Funding for Libraries." *Searcher* 8, no. 1 (January): 51–57.

———. 2006. "Building a New Foundation: Library Funding." *Searcher* 14, no. 1 (January): 26–34.

MacKellar, Pamela H., and Stephanie K. Gerding. 2010. *Winning Grants.* New York: Neal-Schuman Publishers, Inc.

Radford, Jeff. 2011. "Library Boosters Suggest Another Big Explosion." *Corrales Comment*, November 5. http://corralescomment.com/index.php/archive/18-corrales-comment-volume-xxx-no-1-24/1847-library-boosters-suggest-another-big-explosion.

Zabriskie, Christian. 2004. "The Library Fight in Plain Sight." *Huffington Post*, May 14. http://www.huffingtonpost.com/christian-zabriskie/the-library-fight-in-plai_b_5320014.html.

Part III

PROVIDING EFFECTIVE PROGRAMS AND SERVICES AND MEASURING YOUR SUCCESS

CHAPTER 11

Implementing Library Programs and Services

IMPLEMENTATION IS WHEN THE RUBBER MEETS THE ROAD. It is one of the last steps in providing an effective library program or service. This is when you perform the work that makes the program happen.

As you learned in part I, the first steps in providing effective programs and services involve discovering what your users need by assessing and prioritizing current community needs. Once you know the needs in your community, the next step is to determine what programs and services the library will offer to meet their greatest needs.

In part II you learned you must define the goal and objectives of your service, program, or project; identify the activities required to reach the goal and accomplish the objectives; determine who will do the work; calculate how long it will take them to do the work; and allocate the resources they will need to implement the program. You must create a time line and a budget that considers all costs for the program or service and the time it will take to implement from start to finish.

During the planning phase, you develop strategic partnerships with agencies, businesses, organizations, or other libraries that are working to meet the same or similar needs in your community. You obtain buy-in from staff and gain support from administration, municipal leaders, and the larger organization. Only after planning a program or service are you ready to implement it.

◎ Planning First

It is common in the literature about implementing programs for planning to be included as part of the implementation phase. Beware of this paradigm. It is not logical to launch into implementation before you have planned a program or service. As you have learned, a program design changes and evolves as you are planning it. If you are under pressure to plan after you (or someone else) have decided to implement a program, you might rush through the planning part of the process so you can get to work.

You must take adequate time to think through different program design ideas and approaches thoroughly, develop sensible objectives that result in the best outcomes for people, and ensure that the budget covers all the costs. Speedy planning under pressure may result in overlooked partners or important community needs. Deciding to implement before planning is disrespectful to staff. It communicates to them that their input and buy-in are not an important consideration in program planning and implementation.

It is well documented that one of the top reasons for program failure is poor planning (Schlesinger and Farrell 2013). Focusing on implementing at the expense of planning could create miscommunication among staff, a poor reputation for the library in your larger organization, mistrust among the people you serve, loss of credibility among your peers, and bad public relations, to name a few. If your program fails due to poor planning, it will be very difficult to convince staff, administration, partners, and the community to give you another chance in the future. This approach can do serious damage to you and your library, and the resulting ramifications can be difficult to reverse.

Program planning is not a pesky part of implementing a program. It is not something that you have to get out of the way quickly so you can implement a program by a deadline that has been imposed upon you. It is a separate process that is integrally connected to the library's strategic plan and must be completed thoughtfully and thoroughly before implementation. Planning takes time and requires the space to explore different options and approaches. Planning makes providing effective programs and services much easier. It also increases the chances a program will be successful, effective, and meet people's needs. If you want to provide effective library programs and services, planning before implementing is necessary.

◎ Putting Everything in Place

The first order of business is to handle the practical matters that will set the stage for a successful implementation. These include:

- Naming the project, program, or service
- Making a dedicated work space
- Hiring staff
- Creating the team
- Training staff

- Purchasing equipment, materials, supplies
- Updating the time line
- Establishing evaluation baseline

Naming the Project, Program, or Service

If you are implementing a new project in the library, give it a unique and memorable name. You want to attract people and encourage them to take advantage of the library's programs and services. For example, if you are offering computer classes to help people find jobs, you might call the series "Land a Job!" rather than "Computer Training for Unemployed People." Story hours at the Larchmont (New York) Public Library, designed for specific age groups and targeting specific learning topics have names such as "Preschool Palooza," "Young and Restless for Toddlers," and "Itty Bitty Babies" (http://www.larchmontlibrary .org). These programs are likely to spark more interest and participation than one called "Preschool Story Hour."

If you are updating a service you have offered for a while, spruce it up with an updated name. For instance, the term "Reference Service" conjures up a picture of a librarian sitting behind a large desk located near shelves stacked with encyclopedias, dictionaries, fact books, bound journals, and other paper materials. This name is OK; however, if you are adding a new feature such as virtual reference, call attention to it by giving it a unique name. A list of databases on the library's website might be called "Databases," "Virtual Reference Collection," or something unique to your library such as "Springfield Connects."

Giving a name to a program or updating the name to reflect a renewed effort to meet current community needs fosters pride among staff in the work they are doing. It also provides something specific to note when communicating with city leaders, school administrators, or the community about the work you are doing. A new program or service that is folded into an old name will be difficult to feature.

Making a Dedicated Work Space

Establish an area that is dedicated to the program, project, or service. Physical spaces for staff to work in close proximity to one another encourage teamwork, communication, and ownership. The size and configuration of the space depends on the program, the number of staff working on the program, and your library's capacity. For larger projects in larger libraries, this could be a separate office area. For small programs in small libraries, it might be a sign to identify the program; a place for staff to meet; and an area to keep program materials, supplies, and equipment. It is important to recognize the program or service with a separate physical space as this acknowledges the importance of the program, and it provides something tangible that fosters pride among program staff. A physical space represents the work staff members are doing toward a particular goal. When individual library projects, programs, and services are not acknowledged, they tend to disappear into generic "library work."

Hiring Staff

As soon as you are ready to implement a program, hire necessary personnel. Post position advertisements for new staff right away. This could take some time, and until staff is in place, you cannot fully implement the program. If you need consultants, issue RFPs (Requests for Proposals) for the best candidates.

Often, your program staff will consist of existing library staff who will be shifting their work responsibilities from another program or service. This can be difficult for staff who are unfamiliar with the concept of dividing their work time among multiple programs and regularly shifting responsibilities. If you are going to provide effective library programs and services, this means constant change. Staff must get used to working this way to meet current community needs.

Meet in person with these staff members to review their time commitment to your program. Clarify their responsibilities and work hours. Talk about their current work responsibilities that will be assumed by another staff member, and include those staff members in the discussion as well. Everyone must be clear about who is doing what and the hours required to do it. Misunderstandings in this arena can cause great stress and dissatisfaction in the workplace.

If staff changes have occurred since you planned the program, meet with new personnel to introduce yourself, orient them to the program, and clarify their roles. Focus on the program's goal and objectives, and how the program will benefit people. Explain your expectations and consider their strengths when assigning new tasks.

Creating the Team

From the start, choose a team of people who believe in the service, in the importance of meeting the community needs that service is targeting, and improving people's lives in this way. They must be committed and resilient, able to weather the tough times and keep working through difficulties. Hire team players, people who communicate well and complement each other. Look for reliable, motivated personnel who thrive in an environment of mutual respect.

Training Staff

When you are launching a new program or service in your library, it is likely that staff will need training. Prepare them for implementation by providing adequate training in what you expect them to do. You cannot expect staff to perform new tasks without training, nor can you expect them to "pick it up" as they go. Successful library programs and services require knowledgeable staff.

Purchasing Equipment, Materials, Supplies

Acquire the equipment, materials, and supplies you will need to implement the program or service. You many need to purchase technology or expensive equipment that you priced some time ago. Verify prices and, if necessary, make adjustments in the budget. Make these kinds of purchases in a timely manner before prices fluctuate more.

Buy materials and supplies in bulk if possible and do this in the beginning stages of implementation. The workflow will go more smoothly when staff have what they need on site to implement the project.

Updating the Time Line

Using the time line you created in the planning stage, update the activities and fill in gaps by defining additional steps under each activity. Update the personnel responsible for performing each task and define the beginning and ending dates for each activity. The activities happening at the startup are detailed; however, activities planned for later in the project may be less defined. This is fine. You will know more about the details of the later activities as the project unfolds.

The time line provides an essential structure for project implementation. It states the scope of work. It is a tool that allows for cost and time estimates, scheduling and resource requirements. It is a reference for project staff who want a visual picture about the project as a whole and where things currently stand. Post the time line in the work area and update it regularly. Use it in team meetings to update staff and track your progress.

Establishing a Baseline for Evaluation

You must begin evaluation as soon as you start program implementation. It is necessary to establish a baseline or starting point against which you can measure your progress toward achieving the objectives. Without information about where you are starting, any further evaluations will be useless. Decide the best evaluation methodologies for measuring your particular objectives; then, depending on the nature of your program, use the appropriate method to establish the baseline (see chapter 12).

Managing Effective Programs, Projects, and Services

Every library program, project, or service needs a manager, or someone to oversee its implementation. Without someone to oversee and coordinate library programs, services, and projects, it is unlikely they will be effective or successful. Program management involves coordinating, monitoring, and controlling the activities to ensure that the objectives are being met. The primary implementation activities are communication, data collection, and change management (Wamsley 2009).

Program managers have a firm understanding of the details of a program and how it will work, as well as a big picture understanding of program goals, objectives, and outcomes. They understand the need a program or service will meet in the community and how accomplishing the objectives demonstrates that the need is being met. In most cases, the program manager is the person who identified the need, defined the program, collaborated with partners, led the planning effort, and created the time line and budget. When someone has devoted the time and energy necessary to plan a program, she usually has a solid commitment to its success. A person such as this is a good choice for program manager. Appointing someone who has not been involved in program planning to manage a program is not wise.

Program managers usually have the most at stake in the program or service they are implementing, and they are highly committed to seeing it through successfully. They are placed strategically within the organization to manage a particular program or service effectively. The responsibilities are the same whether a librarian manages a project, a program, or a service. Some duties a program manager performs include:

- Overseeing staff and their activities
- Monitoring program evaluation
- Adjusting course and making changes
- Operating within a time frame and budget

- Meeting deadlines
- Monitoring the budget
- Clearly articulating how the program works
- Explaining how the program relates to the role of the library and other library operations
- Answering questions that may arise
- Effectively communicating internally and externally
- Maintaining relationships with partners
- Seeing that the project benefits people by accomplishing goals and objectives
- Acting as a spokesperson for public relations purposes
- Interfacing with the larger organization
- Representing the program in the community

In the planning process, you allocated staff time for the program manager position, provided financial support for it, and identified the activities the program manager will perform. This position is not an afterthought. It should not be a surprise to you at the implementation stage that you need a program manager, nor should you find yourself implementing a program without a manager.

Ⓖ Using Project Management Principles

"Project management is a flexible, mission-oriented management tool that can be used to move both complex and simple projects along" (Anzalone 2000). A widely popular management phenomenon, project management is a process for developing and implementing projects. Books are available on project management, and the Project Management Institute or PMI (http://www.pmi.org/) is devoted to the practice of project management. Courses are offered on project management, and you can earn a degree or certification in this field. Within the available information about basic project management are some important guidelines that librarians would be wise to incorporate in the conception, planning, implementation, and termination phases of library programs, services, and projects.

In the library science literature, attention has been given to project management, focused on the need to manage projects but not programs and services. Some define a project as unique, finite, short-lived, and not recurring. By other definitions, projects have only one goal or purpose, have a defined end to a sequence of activities, operate within a budget, and result in unique outcomes (Fichter 2003). Others contend that projects involve change, are outside the realm of day-to-day activities, have start and end points, and have limitations (Wamsley 2009).

Don't let this terminology confuse you. Don't be fooled into thinking that you do not need to manage programs and services. Library activities do not have to fit into some definition of a "project" to require management. Whether you call a set of collected library activities a "project," a "program," or a "service," it probably needs managing. All library programs and services should have goals and a sequence of activities, not just the short-lived ones. All programs, services, and projects operate within a library's budget, and they all must have objectives and outcomes. Library programs and services that do not involve change are probably not meeting current community needs, and librarians should not be doing them.

To further confuse the issue, the terms "project," "program," and "service" are not used consistently in our field. Furthermore, their definitions are not always clear by their use in practice. Below are some examples:

1. Although the San Francisco Public Library's Project Read is called a project, it is actually a literacy program that offers many services (http://sfpl.org/index. php?pg=0200002801).
2. Stanford University Libraries has innovative projects that involve partnerships with other libraries and companies worldwide, some of which are programs (http://library.stanford.edu/projects).
3. The Toledo-Lucas County Public Library is looking forward to offering additional programs such as medical care for library patrons (Dunn 2015). In another library, this medical care might be called a service.

Ongoing and long-lived library programs and services have the same need to be planned and managed as short-lived and finite ones. For example, reference service is usually considered ongoing, but it still needs a manager to ensure that the service is reaching a goal; accomplishing objectives; meeting current community needs; operating within a budget; is evaluated; adjustments are made to correct ineffective results and improve the service; and reference staff are performing relevant and coordinated activities toward a common goal.

Recurring library services for which you don't know the objectives or outcomes need serious managing. Librarians who have sleep-walked though decades of providing the same generic ongoing library services and programs because they have "always done it that way" should take a very close look at how those services are meeting current community needs. Who is the target audience? What are their needs? What is the goal, what are the objectives, and what are the outcomes for people? How are you evaluating the effectiveness of these services? How are they making a difference for people? How have you changed programs and services over time to adjust to changing current community needs?

Library programs and services that you are not actively managing are likely catatonic. After so many years of offering them because you've always offered them, the idea of planning them to be effective becomes a foreign concept. Don't let this happen in your library. Librarians who have allowed programs and services to go on autopilot have difficulty justifying the library's funding. Do not defer to the more "essential" municipal services for available funding when it is time to fight for the library's budget. Instead, do the work to plan and manage library programs and services. This will not only result in more effective and relevant library activities that benefit people, but it will also give you the knowledge and confidence you need to justify essential library programs and services.

⊚ Communicating and Motivating

A project manager must maintain continuous and clear communication among all the different players, including the project team, administration, and partners. The success or failure of a program, service, or project often depends on effective communication. Before you implement the project, give serious thought to:

- Who needs to know?
- What do they need to know?

- How much do they need to know?
- How often do they need to be informed?

Set up a communication plan that allows you and team members to communicate about the progress of current activities, any problems staff members are encountering, issues they anticipate, and/or technical difficulties they are facing. Clearly explain your communication and decision-making methods. Make it clear the data you will need, when you need it, and by what method. For instance, will you be communicating in person, by phone, or by e-mail? Will you be communicating daily, weekly, or monthly? What do you need to know? For example, you might want to know:

- What have they completed by a certain date?
- What have they not completed and why?
- What are their unsolved problems?

Create distribution lists for communicating with different sets of people. For a small program, you might need one list for project staff, another one for administration, and one for partners. For a complex project, you might need multiple lists for staff working on different aspects of the project, a list for administration and another one for the organization, and several lists for partners and collaborators based on their involvement in different activities and events. You could begin with one list that includes everyone where you will send the work plan or time line upon implementation.

Administration or municipal leaders, key stakeholders, and partners need regular status reports. Keep them informed about your progress and the completed activities. Decide the format for your reports and what data you will report. Be brief, yet informative, and keep the format consistent. You might hold regular status report meetings with program staff in which they can communicate directly with one another about timely issues.

"The real work of teams is done in meetings" (Kern 2014). In-person or face-to-face meetings with staff are essential to communicate effectively. The key to effective meetings is to hold them regularly and to make them specific. Hold a launch meeting when your project is ready to be implemented. Invite everyone involved with the program and explain the work plan. Distribute copies of the plan to those who did not print the one you e-mailed them. This will get everyone on the same page from day one. Clarify the goal or purpose of the program and stress the outcomes or how the community will benefit. Tell anecdotes or personal stories about community members who might benefit and how. If you know of other programs like yours, share their successes with your team. Ask if anyone has questions or if anything needs clarification. Below are some basic ground rules for meetings:

1. Start and end on time
2. Have an agenda
3. State your goals
4. Invite only the people who need to be there
5. Provide work for the meeting
6. Stay on topic
7. Keep meetings to an hour at most
8. Expect everyone to contribute
9. End with actions

In addition to team meetings, it might be appropriate to have one-on-one meetings with staff; one-on-one or group meetings with partners or administration; and community meetings to celebrate milestones. If you are meeting for no reason, don't have the meeting. Program managers lead, facilitate, and motivate teams by:

- Establishing an open environment
- Facilitating learning about each other and their work
- Clarifying the purpose of the project and deliverables
- Encouraging participation and sharing information freely
- Empowering staff to make decisions independently
- Providing structure
- Establishing norms for interacting
- Encouraging open communication
- Fostering trust

Program managers must get buy-in from everyone and focus staff on implementing a successful program. The biggest motivator is a commitment from everyone to make a real difference for people in the community. Explain the project goal and objectives to project staff in terms of outcomes, or how the project will help people. Tell team members that achieving the objectives will meet community needs, and make the connection for them between meeting needs and improving lives. This linear concept is not difficult to understand; yet many librarians have not embraced it down to the program and service level. When staff members understand how even the most mundane and seemingly removed task will contribute to programs and services that help people in a measurable way, they are more likely to be motivated.

A project manager is responsible for moving the team toward accomplishing the project's goal. One simple way to do this is to keep the team focused on the goal at all times. Display the goal in your office, include it in the project's promotional materials, on the website, and in your e-mail signatures. When communicating with staff, continue to make the connection between the mission of the library, community needs, and the goals of the project. This is always a good practice. When you talk about programs and services in terms of how they will benefit people, eventually this will become second nature in the library. Eventually staff will know what outcomes are expected of what programs and services. The days of saying, "We provide that service because we've always provided it" will be over.

Staff members are passionate about programs that make a real difference. They are not deeply inspired to do good work simply for the sake of making the library look good or to accomplish a library director's (or someone else's) dream. When you have designed a program to meet community needs, it will not be difficult to inspire and motivate staff.

Staff members are motivated when you use their individual talents and skills. Take time to interview staff about their strengths and interests; then, use them in implementing the project. Include input from staff about possible adjustments or when troubleshooting challenges. Ask for their ideas and suggestions about better ways to do a task. If someone expresses an interest in learning a new skill, match him or her with a mentor or give him or her the opportunity to shadow a more experienced team member. Program managers also motivate team members by:

- Keeping a positive attitude
- Having confidence in team members

- Listening to team members and supporting them
- Dealing with problems quickly

⑥ Handling Challenges

Unexpected problems are certain to arise during implementation. Common challenges include:

- Budget shortfalls
- Changing partners
- Changing staff
- Technology glitches or failures
- Insufficient staff training
- Failed activity

Monitor your progress and take prompt corrective action on minor issues. Refer to the plan and respond to new information or unforeseen difficulties when they arise. Investigate the cause of the problem or figure out why an activity didn't go as planned. Go back to the goals and objectives and think about other ways to accomplish them. Then adjust the activities to accommodate the unpredicted circumstances.

Operate within a flexible work model and have an alternative work plan ready in case of anomalies. Be prepared to react promptly to major issues and to change course, if necessary. The project manager must be able to do whatever it takes to redirect the project to keep things on track. Be decisive.

Larger problems may require significant changes. Major changes may mean replanning some activities. Modify the action plan if necessary. This will take careful consideration and may ultimately affect the time line and impact the related activities of multiple staff. Keep staff informed throughout this process and seek their input. Things change. As hard as you try, you cannot anticipate everything in advance. It often takes implementing a program to find out how some things will work.

- What is the source of the problem?
- What is the problem?
- What is the benefit of making a change?
- How will the change ensure better outcomes?
- What are the ramifications of doing nothing?
- What is the cost financially?
- What are the alternatives?
- What are consequences and risks of change?
- How will the change impact the objectives and outcomes? (Young)

When you plan and implement programs and services following the steps in this book, you already are decreasing the chances of too many unexpected surprises. Being vision and mission driven will help you to overcome the inevitable obstacles and barriers. Remember where you are headed. Keep your goal, objectives, and outcomes in mind. Don't get mired in the details of the problem. Keep moving forward, stay positive, and seek alternate solutions for meeting people's needs. Act promptly.

As part of the planning process, you researched other projects like yours and incorporated the experiences of others. Repeating mistakes of the past makes no sense. If another library implemented a project like yours and shared its successes and the pitfalls, you had the opportunity to avoid them in your plan. As you face challenges or problems during implementation, refer again to the tips and guidelines prepared by other librarians. They might contain possible solutions to your problem. For instance, ALA's Reference and User Services Association has published *Guidelines for Implementing and Maintaining Virtual Reference Services* (http://www.ala.org/rusa/resources/guidelines/virtrefguidelines), which is meant to assist libraries implementing this service; and Gonzales and Bennett (2014) shared useful tips for effective implementation of a 3-D printing service including where to physically locate the printer and different levels of services.

Even though you have done all the groundwork and prepared well, library staff may exhibit some unexpected resistance. During the planning stage, it is easy for people to agree that change is necessary. Staff may be supportive and encouraging, and they might even offer their expertise or time toward making the change. But when it is time to take action or implement the program, you may become aware for the first time of some reservations. Change is difficult—more difficult for some than for others. Good intentions may fade when reality hits. Be patient and lead them into the future.

Often resistance to change is a result of a lack of understanding about what the project will accomplish. Reiterate the goal and objectives of the project and how it will benefit people. Sometimes personalizing the possible benefits by relating a story or anecdote about how the lives of a person or a family in the community could improve helps resistant team members understand. Once they see that the project will have such a positive impact, they might be convinced that taking a risk is worth it. Ask them to weigh their fear against the possible difference it will make for people with needs. Sometimes shifting the paradigm from focusing on the change to the power to make a difference will encourage staff members who are resistant to change. Some people simply don't want to do the work required of making changes. You must replace those staff members. Do not give power to those who resist change.

⑨ Monitoring Progress and Tracking Expenditures

Implementation involves monitoring and controlling the program's objectives and tasks defined during planning. Establish a system for tracking your progress that allows you to compare the planned activities with the work accomplished. A simple Gantt chart will suffice for smaller time-limited projects involving few staff. Gantt charts show:

- The different activities
- When each activity begins and ends
- How long each activity will last
- Where activities overlap
- Start and end date of the program

To get started, look for a free or inexpensive Gantt chart template for Excel. The example in figure 11.1 was created using a template from ASQ (http://asq.org/learn-about-quality/project-planning-tools/overview/gantt-chart.html). Use the time line from your plan as a starting point for your basic chart. Enter the start and end dates for each activity in addition

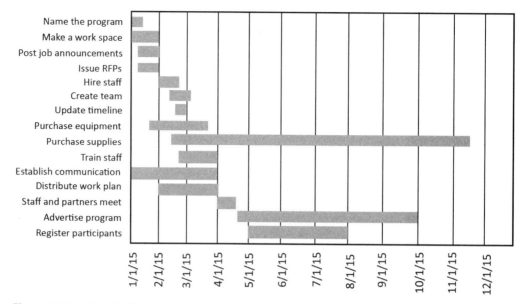

Figure 11.1. Gantt Chart Example.

to making columns for the start and end dates. This visual aid will help you keep abreast of ongoing, upcoming, and completed activities.

Critical Path Method (CPM) is a project management technique that enables program managers to design a schedule, identify critical components, and assign relative importance to each activity. This method brings your time line and Gantt chart to the next level for more complex programs involving more staff.

Computerized ways to keep track of projects include a Word document, an Access database, or an Excel spreadsheet. A web-based tool such as a wiki, free or fee-based web programs, or software could be helpful, depending on the nature of your project. Most software programs are designed to help program managers track multiple activities. When activities run parallel to each other, software can help determine which ones take precedence and allow for adjustments. A manager can slide less important tasks to the side, concentrate on the more urgent ones, and take corrective action quickly. If a crisis occurs, the manager can use the software to implement workarounds.

Free software programs, such as Viewpath (http://www.viewpath.com) or TaskJuggler (http://www.taskjuggler.com), may be suitable for managing some library programs and services. Microsoft Project is a well-known project management program many organizations use. Your larger organization may have a license to a software program that you can use, so check what is available. The nature of your project, program, or service will help determine the appropriate tool.

Successful programs stay within their budgets. To ensure that you are on track, keep records of:

- Time spent on each task
- Resources used on all tasks
- Cost of materials
- Cost of equipment
- Overhead costs
- Cost of staff including benefits

The easiest way to track expenditures is in a spreadsheet such as Excel; however, if you are using program management software, it likely includes a budget module. Use the tools available to you to make sure you are operating within your budget.

If your program or service is new to the library, you may need to update or create new library policies. For instance, in the case of a 3-D printing service, consider what to charge customers, procedures for faulty prints and refunds, priorities for printing jobs, and availability of service (Gonzales and Bennett). Refer to policies that have been tested in libraries with similar programs.

Key Points

By following the process in this book, you already will have planned your program or service carefully before implementing it. This alone will greatly increase your chances of providing an effective program or service. In this chapter, you learned the importance of planning first, what is involved in managing library programs and services, and the role of the program manager in implementing a program.

- Implementation is when you perform the work that makes the program happen.
- Beware of planning as a part of implementation.
- One of the top reasons for program failure is poor planning.
- Every library program, project, or service needs a manager—someone to oversee its implementation.
- Program management involves coordinating, monitoring, and controlling the program activities to ensure that the objectives are being met.
- Program managers usually have the most at stake in the program or service they are implementing, and they are highly committed to seeing it through successfully.
- The success or failure of a program, service, or project often depends on effective communication.
- The biggest motivator is a commitment from everyone to make a difference for people in the community.
- Unexpected problems are certain to arise during implementation.
- Often resistance to change is a result of a lack of understanding about what the project will accomplish.
- Implementation involves monitoring and controlling the program's objectives and tasks defined during planning.

You must consistently and regularly monitor your progress toward accomplishing the project, program, or service's objectives using accepted evaluation methods. The next chapter will cover program evaluation.

References

Anzalone, Filippa Marullo. 2000. "Project Managment: A Technique for Coping with Change." *Law Library Journal* 92, no. 1: 53–70.

Dunn, Ryan. 2015. "Library Considering Expansion of Services, Including Health Care." *Toledo Blade*, January 18. http://www.toledoblade.com/local/2015/01/18/Library-considering-expansion-of-services-including-health-care.html.

Fichter, Darlene. 2003. "Why Web Projects Fail." *Online* 27, no. 4 (July/August): 43–46.

Gonzales, Sara Russell, and Denise Beaubien Bennett. 2014. "Planning and Implementing a 3D Printing Service in an Academic Library." *Issues in Science and Technology Librarianship* (Fall). Doi: 10.50621/F4M043CC.

Kern, Kristine. 2014. "5 Rules for Efficient, Effective Meetings." *Inc.*, April 3. http://www.inc.com/kristine-kern/effective-efficient-meetings.html.

Schlesinger, Kenneth, and Robert Farrell. 2013. *Managing in the Middle: The Librarian's Handbook.* Chicago: American Library Association.

Wamsley, Lori H. 2009. "Controlling Project Chaos: Management for Library Staff." *PNLA Quarterly* 73, no. 2 (Winter): 5–6.

Young, Trevor L. 2013. *Creating Success.* 4th ed. London: Kogan Page.

Measuring Effectiveness

TO ENSURE THE EFFECTIVENESS OF LIBRARY PROGRAMS and services, you must evaluate them. Evaluation means measuring the degree to which your programs are achieving the objectives you aim to accomplish. For example, it means finding out if people learned the information you were teaching, how effectively they use the techniques they learned, or if their new knowledge and skills helped to improve their lives. The days of providing library services and programs simply for the sake of attracting and occupying people are over. Libraries exist to meet community needs; thus library programs and services must make a measurable difference for people in the community.

Evaluation is not mysterious or complicated. It is not reserved for advanced researchers in other fields. A logical way to plan evaluations begins with program planning. When evaluation plans are built into program designs, evaluation simply involves a set of program activities that are supported in the plan along with all of the other program activities. Evaluation is a crucial part of every program and service. It is not an afterthought.

"In order for evaluation to be particularly meaningful, the process requires objectives as criteria" (Matthews 2007, xix). Measuring effectiveness requires first setting out to accomplish specific objectives. The objectives you establish for each program or service during the planning process eventually become the indicators of their success. So when a program or service produces the intended results—or accomplishes its objectives—you can consider it to be effective or successful. Every program and service has a different set of objectives or measures that determine effectiveness in a particular community. One size does not fit all. You must design evaluations that measure specific program or service objectives meant to meet needs in your specific community. Reasons for conducting evaluations include:

- To determine the effectiveness of a program or service
- To track your progress
- To provide the information you need to improve a program or service
- To provide the data you need to make a case for expanding a program or service
- To indicate next steps in meeting community needs
- To illustrate your good track record and help you secure external funding in the future

⊚ Counting, Numbers, and Statistics

Librarians are known for counting many things, including:

- How many people attended a program
- How many books were checked out
- How many people walked through the library doors
- How many reference questions were asked
- How many new materials were purchased
- How many books a child read over the summer

Numbers and statistics are output measures. They are not indicators of effectiveness. "Measures currently reported by public libraries generally do not reflect the outcomes and impact of library services" (Anthony 2014). No correlation exists between increased numbers and increased effectiveness of library programs and services: Big numbers do not indicate the degree to which programs and services are benefiting a community.

Many librarians count things out of habit. They might think that counting things reflects their success because no one has pointed out to them that this is not true. Historically, librarians have kept and protected the books, circulated library materials, regulated materials use, and monitored library attendance. In historical times, it made sense for librarians to count things to justify their worth, but libraries have evolved over the centuries. Today, librarians know that meeting community needs is the impetus for what they do. They know that attendance numbers, numbers of books read, numbers of reference questions asked, and numbers of books circulated are mostly irrelevant when it comes to evaluating effectiveness or outcomes for people.

Unfortunately, some large organizations, municipalities, school districts, university administrations, and state library agencies still require librarians to report statistics about materials, patrons, and library activities as a measure of their success or effectiveness. This way of reporting keeps librarians stuck in the past. They are so busy compiling statistics about what goes on in the library that it is nearly impossible for them to look outside the library to see unmet community needs, or to develop a vision for meeting them. When librarians are stuck in the wrong paradigm and cannot see another approach, change is very difficult.

To conduct useful evaluations, it is essential first to know your library's mission or purpose. Without knowing the library's purpose you cannot determine your priorities or know which programs and services to offer, what you want to accomplish, or how to measure effectiveness. Librarians are very busy people who have many duties and responsibilities. It is easy to get so involved with completing the everyday tasks necessary to keep a library running that librarians sometimes don't stop to think about the library's main purpose. Take time now. Stop and think about it, then answer this question: What is the mission of your library? Is it:

A. To be a very busy place
B. To attract more people into the building
C. To increase attendance at programs and events
D. To circulate more books
E. To solicit more reference questions
F. To get more people to visit the library's website

Or is the mission of your library:

G. To meet people's needs

If you answered yes to A through F, your library's purpose is to increase the level of activity in the library. High activity levels don't say anything about effectiveness. You can have a very busy library with lots of people, high program attendance, skyrocketing circulation numbers, many reference questions, and more clicks on the website without meeting community needs. Librarians cannot afford to operate this way. If your library's mission statement says that the purpose of the library is to be a busy place and circulate lots of books, then it is probably time to convene the board and do some soul searching about how the library might help solve problems in the community instead. With financial support shrinking every year, administrators want to know what you are accomplishing with the funds they are allocating to the library. As money gets tighter, they will ask what you are doing to benefit the community. If you answer that you are providing the same programs and services you have offered for decades because lots of people are attending, the astute ones will eventually redirect the available money to departments that are making a measurable difference in the community, university, corporation, or school district.

If you answered yes to G, then your library is about improving people's lives, and you know that counting things does not demonstrate that. When you focus on meeting community needs as the library's purpose, you won't be fooled by the notion that high numbers mean the library is effective. Library activity levels and benefits for people do not correlate—and thinking they do is irrational. You can increase gate counts in myriad ways that have nothing to do with providing effective programs and services. For instance, you might:

- Ask the local tour bus company to stop at the library and let in all the tourists
- Offer a prize to the person who enters the library the most times in a week
- Provide free day care during story hour
- Serve snacks and drinks to the first hundred people who come in on the first of the month

An article about raising funds for a small village public library in New Mexico cited this proof that the library is "thriving" (Steinberg):

- Library visits have increased 30 percent in five years
- Circulation has jumped 39 percent in the same time period

These statistics are impressive, especially because nationally both library visits and circulation numbers have been trending downward due to the virtual nature of libraries and the availability of electronic materials (Reid 2014). More people are accessing libraries on the web; however, this article makes no mention of the website or use of electronic materials. Nowhere does it say how the library is addressing community needs. Are these numbers enough to evaluate a library's success or determine that it is thriving?

Ultimately, a librarian's job is to know the library's mission and to educate its administrators about libraries in the twenty-first century. This means communicating specifically how the library benefits the community, whether the community is students and faculty in a university, residents in a town or village, students and teachers in a school, or employees in a large corporation or government agency. When the people in power understand the purpose of libraries and specifically what you are doing to improve the lives of people in their communities, they are more likely to support you in doing your work.

Understanding Evaluation Methodologies

To evaluate programs and services you must employ one or more standard evaluation methods that are widely used in many disciplines. In chapter 7 you learned how to develop goals and objectives for a library program or service. Then chapter 8 guided you through how to design programs and services meant to accomplish those specific goals and objectives. When your project design has measurable objectives, evaluations and the methods you use become a natural result of those objectives. Building program and service plans in a logical manner, beginning with assessing community needs, makes evaluation relatively simple to understand. Every program plan should include an evaluation plan.

The most appropriate evaluation method is the one that yields the strongest data to measure the particular goals and objectives of the program or service you are evaluating. You may use more than one method to evaluate a single program or service. You will likely use different methodologies to evaluate different programs and services. One evaluation method will not be appropriate for evaluating all programs and services. Evaluation is an entire discipline of its own. This chapter provides an overview; however, you can investigate the many books, articles, and courses on evaluation. Librarians must use established and proven evaluation tools and methodologies to measure the effectiveness of library programs and services.

Quantitative Data and Qualitative Data

In general, you have available two broad methodologies to gather information about library services and programs: quantitative and qualitative. Quantitative data are numerical and report the quantity of something. They are used to predict or estimate the outcome of something, or diagnose the current state of a project. Most librarians are familiar with quantitative data because they are accustomed to reporting library activity in numbers. Examples of quantitative methods include:

1. Counting
2. Surveys and questionnaires

Qualitative data are narrative. They report the quality or character of something, such as a user's experience. They are concerned with insight, or the recognition of patterns and connections. Qualitative data capture the thoughts, feelings, attitudes, and behaviors of individuals and help explain why and how. Examples of qualitative methods include:

- Case studies
- Documentation review
- Interviews
- Focus groups
- Observation

Surveys and Questionnaires

You can gather a great deal of information quickly and easily from many people by administering questionnaires and surveys. You can create them inexpensively and distribute them at a relatively low cost in a short time to many people. You can distribute written surveys in paper format or electronically on the web, or conduct oral surveys in person or by telephone. Surveys and questionnaires consist of predefined questions and answer choices. Everyone responds to the same instrument. Most people are familiar with how to complete surveys, and surveys are usually nonthreatening when people can submit them anonymously. The shorter a survey, the more likely people will complete and submit it. You can ask many kinds of questions on a survey:

- Factual
- Opinion or attitude
- Self-perception
- Information
- Standards of action
- Projective
- Past or present behavior

And you can format questions in multiple ways:

- Multiple choice
- Checklists
- Fill in the blanks
- Scaled
- Open-ended

It is important to ask only the questions that will help you determine whether you achieved the goal and objectives of a program or service. Asking irrelevant questions or asking about things you don't intend to address decreases a respondent's confidence in the survey. Use simple, straightforward language and be clear about what you are asking. Survey results are fairly straightforward to gather, compare, and analyze. You should use a questionnaire or survey:

- When you want a participant's perspective
- When you have limited time, personnel, and/or money
- When you want to gather information anonymously

Surveys are subjective. They measure what a respondent perceives to be true. For instance, if you want to know if a class participant has more confidence using an online service after having taken a class on how to use it, a survey question is appropriate. However, a survey will not measure how much the participant's knowledge or skill level has changed as the result of a class.

CUSTOMER SATISFACTION SURVEYS *DO NOT* MEASURE PROGRAM SUCCESS

Beware of using customer satisfaction surveys as evaluation tools. Unless your program's objectives are to provide an easy-to-find location, comfortable furniture, or polite librarians, do not ask questions such as "Was the library easy to find?" "Is the library furniture comfortable?" or "Was the librarian polite?" Do you plan to move the library, buy new furniture, or fire impolite librarians depending on the survey results? Ask only questions that will measure your program's specific objectives and those you intend to address. Customer satisfaction surveys can be helpful when you want to know if library users are generally happy with the library.

Interviews

Interviews will help you understand more fully someone's impressions or experiences of a program or service. They help provide a better understanding of a situation from the point of view of the library customer. They can be conducted in person or via technology such as telephone, videoconference, or online. When you talk with someone, you have the opportunity to get the full range and depth of the information he is sharing. You can develop a rapport with the interviewee, ask for clarification, and be flexible with your questions. Interviews provide subjective data, and they may reveal opinions that don't reflect the true success of a program or service. Analyzing interview data is a very time-consuming process; however, interviewing may yield future partners and new ideas. Interviews can add valuable information for outcome-based assessments because they are likely to indicate changes in a person's behavior, attitude, skill, life condition, or knowledge. You should use interviews:

- When you want more information or you want people to elaborate on answers
- When you want to be flexible
- When you are interested in opinions
- When you want to develop relationships with interviewees

Interviews can be expensive because someone must devote concentrated time and attention to interacting with each participant. In addition, interviews must be carefully recorded, transcribed, coded, and analyzed.

Focus Groups

Focus groups are group discussions conducted in person to gain information about participants' views on a program or service, or their reactions to them. It is necessary to have a moderator with strong leadership and interpersonal skills to manage a focus group. Interactions within the group may disclose perceptions, attitudes, and points of view in a friendly, relaxed, and comfortable atmosphere. Focus groups can provide useful honest information through comments and discussion about shared experiences, and they can help clarify common criticisms.

Focus groups are an efficient way to get key information about a narrowly defined service or program. The topics and questions need to target the community or group rather than the individual. Focus groups can be the right method to help clarify results from a survey, questionnaire, or test; however, focus groups are not useful for measuring an individual's progress or achievements (Rubin 2006). Similar to interviews, a recorder records the proceedings and gathers the focus group data by taking notes. Analyzing focus group data can be expensive and time consuming, although data mining software programs can assist with identifying common themes in both focus groups and interviews. You should use focus groups:

- When you want open-ended opinions
- When you want fresh ideas and responses
- When you want shared impressions on a community or individuals

Observation

You can gather information about how a service or program operates by observing it in action. For instance, you can observe a reference interview or a technology training session for the effectiveness of the reference librarian or technology trainer, or the person's ability to interact with patrons and participants. Observation is often used in conjunction with another evaluation method to clarify or verify results. It can help you determine whether you need to make adjustments in the operation to facilitate effectiveness. You should use observation:

- When you want to view operations of a program as it is happening
- When you want to adapt or adjust programs in process

Documentation Review

By reviewing documents such as applications, memos, financial statements, training manuals, and communications, you can get an impression of how the program is operating without interrupting the program itself. You might need information that another agency or school district has already collected. For instance, if a library program seeks to help students maintain their reading levels over the summer, school records from the spring and fall for individual students may provide the information you need. You should use documentation review:

- When you want to get comprehensive and historical information
- When you want to gather unbiased information
- When you want to accumulate facts about processes

Tests

Pretests and posttests will tell you what individuals learned in a class or training session. They are invaluable for measuring the knowledge gained in a class. Tests can be written, oral, or performance-based; and formats are usually multiple choice, completion, true/false, and rating scale. The cost for tests is relatively low, and commercial training modules often come complete with pretests and posttests. You should use tests:

- When you want to assess whether individuals gained knowledge in a class or training session
- When you want to measure how much of some specific information individuals learned

Choosing the Right Evaluation Methods

The evaluation methodologies you use can be very simple or very complex depending on the nature of the program or service and the outcomes you expect. The best method is the one that will answer the questions you want answered with the resources you have available.

Step 1: Read the objective.
For example, 90 percent of participants will know how to use the library's JobNow service to create a résumé.

Step 2: Determine what question(s) you must ask to measure your success in achieving the objective.
The question you need to answer is, "Do you know how to use JobNow to create a résumé?"

Step 3: Decide the kind of data you need to collect and the methods for collecting the data.
For instance, administer a knowledge test (quantitative) or ask a yes/no question on a survey or questionnaire (qualitative).

Step 4: Decide which method is best.
The survey question will yield a subjective opinion. A participant could answer "yes" when he perceives he could create a résumé but he actually cannot. The knowledge test will tell you whether he can actually create a résumé. In this case, the test will give you the answer you need to measure your success. When 90 percent of participants can demonstrate by successfully taking a test to complete a résumé, you will have achieved the objective.

As you have learned, all programs, services, and projects are designed to meet needs by accomplishing measurable objectives. When your program or service has objectives, it is not difficult to determine the appropriate evaluation method(s). Every service, program, and project likely has multiple objectives. It is important to work through each objective separately to determine which evaluation method(s) are appropriate. Read the many available articles and books on this topic in the library science literature. Be flexible and creative about how you evaluate a service within the parameters of acceptable evaluation methodologies. Insist on measuring your effectiveness accurately and honestly as a function of the objectives you have set out to accomplish. Don't take shortcuts. Keep it simple.

Evaluation is a simple concept for librarians who have planned programs and services to meet specific community needs. They know what they are trying to accomplish and they have determined the markers that will help them see their progress. The problem arises when you have no defined objectives against which to measure your progress. Librarians who offer programs and services without objectives are often confused, defensive, or resistant to the idea of evaluating programs and services. This is understandable. When a program has no objectives, this means you are not expecting to accomplish anything, and it is difficult to admit that you offer programs and services that are not meant to accomplish anything.

Revisit your programs and services to ensure that they have specific, measurable, and time-bound objectives. If they don't, take the time to go back to planning. If you have not assessed community needs or designed programs and services to meet those needs, you will be lost when it comes to evaluation. Conducting needs assessments and planning programs and services to meet community needs are required if you want to conduct meaningful evaluations and ultimately make a difference in people's lives.

◎ Organizing, Tabulating, and Analyzing the Data

Before you begin to organize the data, review your program's goals and objectives. This will ground you in why you are doing the evaluation and help you focus on relevant results. If you are working with quantitative data, you will likely be tabulating the results. Start by organizing the data by topic or main objective. For instance, if you want to determine how many participants gained knowledge or learned something, you might organize and record data from pretests and posttests in a chart or a spreadsheet program. If you ask a "yes" or "no" question on a survey, you will add the number of "yes" responses, the "no" responses, then report the percentages. For ranking questions, you could compute an average for each question and report the results as percentages. Let the objectives guide you as you organize and analyze your results.

If you are working with qualitative information such as a focus group recording, you might first make a form that includes all of the categories or issues discussed with columns for concerns, suggestions, recommendations, and so forth. Depending on the specifics of your objectives, you might make accommodations for breaking down the responses by age group, geographic location, or economic status, for example. As you listen to the recording, you might notice common themes that could suggest creating subcategories. Always remember what you are measuring to avoid becoming distracted by irrelevant remarks. Again, the objectives will tell you what you need to analyze and report. Refer any written or verbal comments that don't relate to your program to the appropriate staff person. They should be addressed in another way.

Because you have included evaluation costs in the program's budget, you should not expect extra costs or surprises at this point. If they appear, take a close look at the evaluation costs in the budget and make sure you understand why you failed to estimate correctly. It is necessary for you to bring this knowledge forward into the planning of future programs and services. The goal is to be able to prepare an accurate budget in the planning stage that includes evaluation costs. Avoid adding evaluation to project activities at the conclusion of a project or as an afterthought. Evaluation must be a part of planning every program and service from the beginning.

It is unrealistic to hire a professional evaluator to evaluate all library programs and services; however, if the larger organization has a professional evaluator on staff, whenever possible use this person's expertise. Librarians must embrace evaluation as an important aspect of librarianship and build it into their work. As librarians learn how to do this, they will understand how to employ the tools and instruments available to them, and how to use volunteers, members of the friends' group, or student workers to assist.

⌾ Communicating Your Results

Librarians must communicate how library programs and services are making a difference, and how the community is benefiting. They must be prepared to "prove" results or measure success with meaningful data. Simply saying the library is a cozy place where people like to go is not a valid strategy for securing continued funding in the twenty-first century. The idea that "everyone loves libraries" so therefore they should be adequately funded is not an intelligent talking point. Remember, statistics and numbers alone do not prove success. Instead, let others know about your accomplishments by using evaluation data to show benefits for people.

Disseminate results internally and externally (Rubin 2006). The nature and size of the program, project, or service will dictate to whom and how. For instance, for larger one-time projects that were grant funded, write a report to the funding agency. Tailor the report for each audience, and distribute it to partners and collaborators. The key to communicating results lies in determining the information an administrator, stakeholder, or funder wants to know about your effectiveness and presenting it in an easy-to-understand format that has an impact. Talk to your audience first and determine their interests and priorities. Customize the information you will present and use a format that will answer their questions. Be prepared with facts using the data.

Issue press releases and newsletter articles to spread the news about effective results. Include stories and anecdotes to convey personalized experiences of individual community members. Regularly communicate evaluation results for ongoing services and programs to staff, administrators, and the library board in an easy-to-read chart or table format. When community benefits are significant or large changes occur from previous years, communicate the information to local news agencies and your larger organization.

⌾ Using Evaluation to Move Forward

"Defining success is not a destination but a journey, and the definition of success will change over time as the library meets and exceeds its goals" (Matthews 2007, 332).

Determine whether you have met the program's objectives by comparing the evaluation results with the objectives. You either have met the objectives or failed to meet them. If you have successfully achieved your objectives, celebrate and congratulate yourself and your staff. You have done your jobs well. Meet with program staff and debrief. Internal adjustments may be needed beyond what the evaluation results reveal. Make the adjustments and continue with the program if it is ongoing. Stretch yourselves by creating objectives in the future that are more challenging, or add new components to the program to meet changing community needs.

If you have not achieved an objective, ask why. Seek answers for how to make the program more effective in the future by carefully examining your evaluation results. You may need to follow up with participants by holding interviews, focus groups, or observing the program in action to find answers. Sometimes a program or service needs to be implemented more efficiently. It may require major adjustments in terms of the activities or resources allocated. If you came close to achieving the objectives, they might only need fine-tuning to be realistic. It is possible that the program activities did not address the objectives very well. You may need to revisit and adjust the program plan. Make the necessary adjustments. Be realistic. Meet with program staff and brainstorm possible solutions. Make strategic decisions about next steps.

You might conclude that a program needs to be eliminated altogether because you cannot see a way to meet the objectives with that particular program. Possibly your objectives were too ambitious. You might see that you were unrealistic and that it is unlikely the program will be a success with the existing objectives. It is a good thing to know when a program isn't making a difference. Use what you have learned to create a new and improved realistic program that will meet needs. Failure is an opportunity to get it right. You must know why you failed in order to make changes or move forward. Library resources must be allocated—or reallocated—to the most relevant services and programs that are making a difference. You don't want funds going to a failing program, and some programs fail. That is a fact.

Discontinuing some library programs and services to make way for more effective ones can be revolutionary in libraries that have stagnated due to the perception that some programs and services must be offered in the future because they were always offered in the past. The idea that programs and services can be redesigned, downsized, or eliminated when they become inefficient or irrelevant liberates some library staff. Evaluation allows librarians to move forward and gives them the freedom to plan and design new, innovative programs and services that will make a difference in their communities. It connects librarians to the community in a meaningful way. Creative, vibrant librarians who are willing to take a risk so people can benefit want to work in libraries that evaluate programs and services. Without evaluation you have no way to know if what you are doing is making a difference.

Libraries have come a long way. They are no longer warehouses for books, and librarians do more than count the books and the people reading them. Librarians these days provide programs and services that meet changing community needs. With needs constantly changing, library programs and services must also change in libraries where the purpose is to meet community needs. Change is what makes librarianship an exciting and dynamic profession. Librarians always have something new to do, and it is usually changing. It is not smart (or interesting) to do the same things over and over because you have always done them that way. This is the easy way out if you don't have objectives or if you don't know why you are doing what you are doing. If you don't evaluate what you are doing, you are likely to keep doing what you have always done, even if it is not working.

Don't be a librarian who says, "We've always done it that way" (Stephens). When you say this, you are announcing to the world that you are satisfied doing the same things over and over, you are not concerned with meeting the community's changing needs, and you don't evaluate what you do. It is time for all librarians to think about how to demonstrate their effectiveness by measuring meaningful results. Evaluation is not a new concept within or outside libraries. We can use decades of research and experience as a foundation. Evaluation not only measures effectiveness, but it also gives you the information you need to improve library programs and services by adjusting or altering activities, staff, budgets, or time lines, for instance.

For many years articles have appeared in the library science literature about a new approach for librarians to measure the effectiveness of library services. PLA's (Public Library Association's) Performance Measurement Task Force is in the process of developing a new set of standardized outcome measures for public libraries. Carolyn A. Anthony, *PLA Online* editor, describes outcome measurement as a "new way" to demonstrate effectiveness (Anthony 2014). This is a very encouraging development for public libraries; however, librarians must know how to use common evaluation methodologies to develop customized instruments that measure the effectiveness of their library's specific programs and services. Evaluation is not a one size fits all discipline.

Avoid distributing a standardized generic survey to measure the effectiveness of a library program that intends to meet a specific need unique to your community. This is a waste of time and energy. If you are going to conduct evaluations, make sure you measure accurately the effectiveness of your specific programs and services against their defined objectives.

ⓖ Key Points

You must evaluate library services and programs to ensure their success. Measuring the degree to which your programs are achieving the objectives you aim to accomplish is essential if you are going to make a difference for your community.

- Evaluation is a crucial part of every program and service. It is not an afterthought.
- The objectives you establish during the planning process for each program or service eventually become the indicators of their success.
- Numbers and statistics are output measures; they do not indicate effectiveness.
- To conduct useful evaluations, it is essential first to know your library's mission or purpose.
- When your project design has measurable objectives, evaluations and the methods you use become a natural result of those objectives.
- The most appropriate evaluation method is the one that yields the strongest data to measure the particular goals and objectives of the program or service you are evaluating.
- Library resources must be allocated—or reallocated—to the most relevant services and programs that are making a difference.
- Evaluation allows librarians to move forward and gives them the freedom to plan and design new and innovative programs and services that will make a difference in their communities.
- Librarians must embrace evaluation as an important aspect of librarianship and build it into their work.

- Let others know about your accomplishments by using evaluation data to show benefits for people.
- If you don't evaluate what you are doing, you are likely to keep doing what you have always done, even if it is not working.

It is important to evaluate programs and services continuously with a goal of making all you do more effective. Chapter 6 (see figure 6.1) explained that evaluation is the last step in designing library services and programs; however, the process doesn't stop here. The next chapter covers how to move forward by incorporating an ongoing process of providing programs and services your community needs into your work.

References

Anthony, Carolyn A. 2014. "Moving Toward Outcomes." *Public Libraries Online* (Public Library Association), July 7. http://publiclibrariesonline.org/2014/07/moving-toward-outcomes/.

Matthews, Joseph R. 2007. *The Evaluation and Measurement of Library Services.* Westport, CT: Libraries Unlimited.

Reid, Ian. 2014. "2013 Public library Data Service Statistical Report: Characteristics and Trends." *Public Libraries Online*, May 9. http://publiclibrariesonline.org/2014/05/2013-plds/.

Rubin, Rhea Joyce. 2006. *Demonstrating Results: Using Outcome Measurement in Your Library.* Chicago: American Library Association.

Steinberg, David. 2014. "Corrales Gallery to Raise Funds for Library Building." *Albuquerque Journal*, March 15. http://www.abqjournal.com/369317/news/corrales-gallery-to-raise-funds -for-library-building.html.

Stephens, Michael. 2014. "Always Doesn't Live Here Any More." *Library Journal*, October 21. http://lj.libraryjournal.com/2014/10/opinion/michael-stephens/always-doesnt-live-here- anymore-office-hours/.

CHAPTER 13

Using Your Success to Move Forward

IN THIS CHAPTER

▷ Leveraging the natural benefits

▷ Using a continuous improvement model

▷ Securing funding

▷ Marketing the library

▷ Moving forward

Providing Library Programs and Services that meet community needs is an ongoing process. Librarians who are focused on communities continuously evaluate programs and services with a goal of making all they do more effective. They may add or subtract activities, shift staff responsibilities, adjust program objectives, eliminate some services altogether, or add others, for instance. The idea is to meet people's changing needs consistently by constantly adjusting what you are doing. Once you start, you won't want to stop. When you finish planning a program, to lock it in for the next few decades "as is" is not an option. Remember, this outdated practice has driven many libraries into a ditch.

Librarians who take this path are committed to a new way of working. Although it may be a big adjustment in the beginning, in the end it is easier and makes more sense than the old ways. It becomes clear that it is more rewarding to address current community needs directly than to offer stale, obsolete programs that originated decades ago when the community had very different needs. It is so enjoyable to work in the present, experiencing direct results, you will wonder why it took so long to look at things this way.

ⓖ Leveraging the Natural Benefits

Natural benefits will become apparent right away, including a renewed passion for work, a revitalized workplace, positive feedback from the community, visible results, and better positioning for funding. Planning programs and services with a fresh look at current needs and considering new ways for the library to fulfill its role results in a confidence and fresh enthusiasm about the possibilities for the library and its potential to make a difference.

Seeing measurable results gives librarians a deeper understanding of the benefits the library can create for their communities, and they realize their power to make a difference. You will see the results in action as programs and services improve people's lives in tangible ways. Once you experience the benefits, it will be impossible to go back to the old ways of providing the programs and services you have always offered because you weren't sure how to do things differently.

A different segment of the population will begin to use the library and the website. You will start to hear about their needs. You will realize that serving the same people you have served for years is not what you are about. New and exciting possibilities will present themselves. Your enthusiasm for work will grow, and it will be contagious. Coworkers will join you in the excitement, and they will be eager to participate in this new approach. Staff will work more efficiently with less wasted time. They will know why they are doing what they are doing. They will take more pride in their work. Every task will have a purpose that is connected to making a difference for people. They will be eager to participate on new planning teams.

Librarians who are community-focused manage more smartly, and they know exactly what they need to be more effective. They are nimble and respond quickly. They are able to manage program-based budgets more effectively. Shifting money to improve services becomes logical and justifiable. No more generic never-ending lamenting about the library's lack of money, being short-staffed, and all the things the library needs. Everything purchased will be related to how it will make a difference for people. Library staff will work effectively within their means. Everyone will know how and where to seek additional funding for necessary programs and services.

All staff will be more involved in the community; the library will become a real stakeholder, and an attractive potential partner for other agencies, schools, departments, and organizations. Directors, staff, and board members will be more aware of what others are doing to serve community needs, and everyone will actively work to collaborate with others.

ⓖ Using a Continuous Improvement Model

Established frameworks in other fields will help ground you in a larger context as you begin to work this way. Because not many librarians have ventured here, it may be challenging at times to stand your ground. You might be tempted to sink back into your old ways because most librarians around you think this way.

Continuous improvement, established by W. Edwards Deming after World War II, is a model that can help you visualize what you are doing in a larger context. It is a systems approach that has been successfully applied in business, industry, education, and government that focuses on improving organizational processes. Librarians have been slow to adapt these principles, even though people in other professions have used them successfully for decades to improve their effectiveness. "After a flurry of interest in the 1990s, interest waned [in libraries], perhaps because traditional structures were deeply imbedded and the impetus to change had not reached a crisis point" (Laughlin and Wilson 2008, 4).

Continuous improvement incorporates the ongoing examination of organizational processes. The idea is to discover and eliminate problems, thus improving processes. For our purposes, use this model to illustrate continuous examination of the processes involved in providing effective programs and services. This concept will encompass all library work.

The paths to continuous improvement are numerous; however, the four-step PDSA (Plan-Do-Study-Act) quality model is easily adaptable to the way of working described here. This model is sometimes called the Deming Cycle or Shewart Cycle (see figure 13.1). The steps, their meaning, and references to chapters in this book appear in table 13.1.

Refer to this model as you work to make programs and services more effective. Beware of library literature that presents this model in terms of continuously improving library processes such as cataloging books. Stay focused on meeting community needs. Do not revert to focusing on the time it takes to catalog a book or the number of children at story hour. This will put you right back into the old way of operating. Your goal is to make programs and services more effective, not to streamline library processes. This can be challenging because librarians have been indoctrinated to think about what happens in the library and measuring it to determine effectiveness. You must be persistent and confident to break with this old thinking.

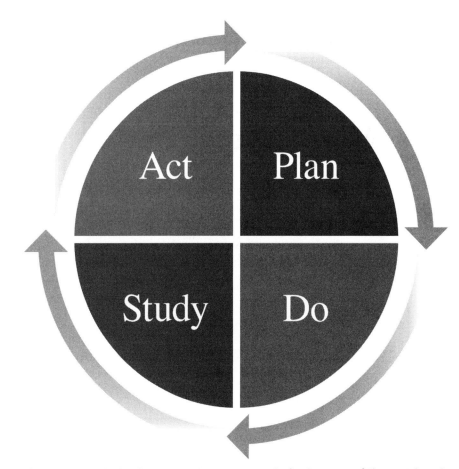

Figure 13.1. PDSA Continuous Improvement Cycle. Courtesy of The W. Edwards Deming Institute.

Table 13.1. Continuous Improvement Cycle: Steps, Meanings, and Book References

STEP	MEANING	BOOK REFERENCE
PLAN	Identify community needs and plan how to meet them.	Chapters 4–5 and Part II
DO	Implement the plan.	Chapter 11
STUDY	Evaluate the program or service. Use data to analyze the results or degree of the change, and determine whether it has made a difference.	Chapter 12
ACT	If the change was successful, implement it on a wider scale and continue to assess results. If it did not work, go back to PLAN and make necessary adjustments to ensure success.	Part II

This model allows directors and staff to identify and change the parts of a program or service that need improvement. This is good, because rarely do you get everything right the first time. The basic idea of being effective is to assess needs continuously, implement programs to meet them, make adjustments, evaluate results, and take action—or Plan-Do-Study-Act. When you do this, you will always know what you need to be more effective.

If you lose your focus, read the library's mission statement as a reminder about what you are doing. Chances are the mission statement addresses how the library will serve the community, not that the library will catalog books more quickly or attract bigger crowds to movie nights.

⊚ Securing Funding

One challenge that comes with providing effective programs and services is funding them. Librarians are very familiar with funding issues, so this will not come up suddenly when you are more effective. In fact, it will be much less work to maintain or secure funding when your programs are effectively meeting community needs versus pleading for money to buy the things the library needs.

It is almost certain that you will not have all the funding you need to provide the programs and services necessary to meet community needs. When you use a program budget (see chapter 9), you will have the ability to move funds around to maximize your efforts. Your first plan should be to find the necessary funds in your regular budget. Money could be hiding in ineffective programs. Beyond this, you may find it necessary assertively to pitch your programs and services that lack sufficient funding in a local budget meeting. You may also need to seek alternative funding or grants from the government or private foundations.

If librarians are going to compete with others for funding, they must be able to demonstrate how they improve people's lives by meeting their needs. The reality is that the people in charge of distributing money in communities, schools, colleges, corporations, governments, and private foundations always carefully scrutinize their choices. They all want to give the money where it will make the most difference in people's lives.

Organizational or Local Funding

Libraries are funded differently, depending on their type. Public, school, academic, and special librarians alike have a huge advantage when it comes to funding if they are community-focused, or centered on meeting the needs of the people they serve. When you work this way, you will have data, success stories, and proof that you are making a difference in very specific ways. You will be able to answer questions from funders quickly and respond to challenges without a second thought. You will know your programs and services inside and out, and you will be able to explain confidently how they benefit the community. When asked to defend the library's budget or justify a request for additional funding, you will be able to answer quickly. You will not find yourself leafing through pages of statistics, trying to come up with something relevant. What you do will take on the importance it deserves in the eyes of those with the money.

When a director can demonstrate the library's effectiveness by presenting data to prove that people's lives have changed or improved as a result of library programs and services, she can confidently compete for funding. Don't go silent when you need to make a case for library funding. Instead, be prepared. If you know how the library benefits the community in measurable ways, you can debate with others about the funding the library needs and why. Saying the library deserves the money because libraries are "good" or "everyone loves libraries" is not a valid argument. Do not defer to more "essential" departments when you are proposing the budget. If the library is working to meet community needs, it *is* essential.

IS YOUR LIBRARY ESSENTIAL?

Once there was a small public library where the funding was always tight. The Friends of the Library funded all of the children's programs, and adult programs didn't exist at all. The director distributed customer satisfaction surveys to members of the friends and regular library users, and called it a community needs assessment. She was very focused on what was going on inside the library and on the more affluent library users who were in her social circle. Many community residents never came to the library. They had many unmet information needs; however, the library director didn't notice them because she was so focused on what was going on inside the library and the positive feedback from the customer satisfaction survey. She was happy that the people she knew were satisfied with the library. One day she attended an important meeting of department heads where town funding for the upcoming year was on the agenda. Upon her return, a staff member asked her how it went. She responded that other departments such as police and fire came out ahead because they provided "essential" services. She said the library wasn't essential, so she didn't speak up. She didn't realize that the library might have been essential if meeting community needs was a concern. She couldn't make a case for the library's value because in her way of thinking it had none.

Grants or Alternative Funding

Librarians who already know their community's needs, the library's program and service designs, and what funding they need to implement them have a big advantage when seeking grants and alternative funding. The information and data generated as a result of working to provide effective programs and services produces components that most grant proposals require. This will save time when it comes to applying for grants or alternative funding. Librarians who work this way will be prepared and ready to respond quickly and confidently to grant announcements. Being prepared increases the chances of winning grants. Many librarians say they don't apply for grants because it is too much work. It is not too much work if you are already planning programs and services to meet community needs effectively. In this case, you are already doing the work. For instance:

1. Grant research is more efficient because you will be able to search for specific funders and grants that fund programs such as yours, or those that fund the elements needed for your particular program or service.
2. A Statement of Needs is usually required in proposals for funding. You will have a community profile and results from a recent community needs assessment ready to include in a proposal. Applicants who demonstrate that they are focused on community needs have an advantage.
3. You will have prioritized the needs and created program designs. The designs include program goals, measurable objectives, activities, staff requirements, budgets, time lines, and evaluation plans. These are all common requirements in grant proposals that you will have ready to go into an application.
4. You will have partners and collaborators in place already because they have been involved since the assessment and planning phases. Collaboration is the key to being successful with grants.
5. Staff members who are experienced in providing effective programs and services are assets.
6. You already will have buy-in from library staff and administration.
7. Use the data you have from providing effective programs and services to demonstrate what funding you require. This illustrates to funders that you are credible, you know how to implement and manage a program, and you know that the funding will make a difference. Funders want to have confidence in you, your library, and your program before they give you money to continue or expand. They want to make a difference.

Governments and private foundations that grant alternative funding to organizations, agencies, academic institutions, schools, and municipal departments are faced with the same choices. They give money to those that will make the most difference. Proposals that do not present programs or services that meet needs or solve problems fail to rise to the top.

⊚ Marketing the Library

Let others know what you are doing and how you are doing it. When you are passionate about your work and the difference you are making, you naturally want tell others about your success. You will informally share information about how the people in your community are benefiting. Take the extra step and contact local media about a notable success. Send press releases about new programs and successful services. Be visible. Newspapers and television are often looking for positive news stories to offset the usual negative news. Highlight the community members who benefit rather than the library itself. Share success stories and include anecdotes. Keep your focus on the community.

Community members who benefit from library programs and services will tell others about how you improved their lives. You will start to notice people in your community who might benefit the most from what the library can offer, and you will become excited at the prospect of addressing more needs in the future. Different people may start coming to the library as you attract nonusers.

Market the library by advertising your successes internally. Write articles for the town employees' paper, school or university e-news, or company intranet. Remember, you want to reach far enough to let the people who don't use the library know that you are interested in their needs, too. Don't perpetuate the myth that informing library users or friends' groups about what you are doing is effective marketing to your community.

Your peers will ask how you are making such great things happen for your community. Share your approach freely. Write an article for a library publication, write a blog post, or present a session at a library conference to introduce others to this way of thinking and working. You will wonder why most librarians aren't seizing the same opportunity. Probably they don't know about it, or they haven't heard about this paradigm. Possibly some are so averse to change that they cannot even consider a new approach. Unfortunately, some librarians will not be receptive at all. They may never have been required to focus on their communities, and they are not about to start now. Some administrators and state library agencies accept statistics as proof that the library is thriving, so some librarians see no reason to do things differently.

It is the responsibility of librarians who understand the benefits of this approach for both communities and libraries to explain the process in simple terms. For instance, when you see community needs assessment training advertised that describes measuring staff performance and program attendance as a way of assessing the community, because you know better it is your responsibility to speak up. When you hear another librarian talk about distributing a customer satisfaction survey to everyone who walks into the library, gently inquire about the needs of the rest of the community. Sometimes a simple question will spark an educational moment.

Once the word spreads you will find library staff, community members, staff from other departments and agencies, and local business leaders stepping forward to ask how they can participate. Potential partners and collaborators may emerge unexpectedly with proposals about working together. You will find that many alternative funding opportunities are available for programs and services that change people's lives.

Moving Forward

A flourishing and valued, vibrant and relevant library is one where librarians and others who do the work of the library are attuned to the community and what people need. Library staff will share a passion for fulfilling the library's mission and for providing relevant programs and services for the betterment of the community. An effective library is one where librarians stay informed about new technological developments as well as being aware of demographic shifts in their communities. It is one where librarians continuously adjust and carefully plan programs and services to meet changing needs while simultaneously incorporating emerging technological innovations.

Important, significant issues are facing our country and our world. Librarians have the unusual opportunity to step up to the plate as leaders of information, knowledge, and learning. This is no time to lurk in the background, offering the same programs and services you have offered for decades because you have always offered them. It is time to venture into the community and actively engage. Find out what people need. Reach out to the people who don't use the library, as they are an important part of the community who may have the greatest unmet needs.

Librarians bring unique skills and a broad range of possibilities to the table. Their skills and strengths can be used in new, exciting, and meaningful ways. Librarians are viable partners and potential collaborators in cities, schools, colleges, and organizations. They can be part of the solution. When librarians are willing to take a risk, step into new territory, and take on new roles, they can be a driving force in their communities, colleges and universities, schools, and corporations.

If libraries are to survive, the alternative is not an option. Libraries can be driving forces, representing the leading edge in information, knowledge, and learning in their communities, colleges and universities, schools, and corporations. For this to happen, librarians must lead the way, they must adapt quickly to change, and they must have a vision for the evolving role of libraries by meeting community needs.

Key Points

To meet people's changing needs consistently you must constantly adjust what you are doing. This is an ongoing cycle that has no end point. Natural benefits to working this way include a renewed sense of purpose, new funding opportunities, and marketing the library.

- Providing effective programs and services that meet community needs is an ongoing process.
- Working this way results in a renewed passion for your work, a revitalized workplace, positive feedback from the community, visible results, and better positioning for funding.
- When you are community-centered, potential partners and collaborators may emerge with proposals about working together.
- A continuous improvement model such as PDSA can help you visualize the process as you provide effective programs and services.
- Public, school, academic, and special librarians alike have a huge advantage when it comes to funding if they are community-focused, or centered on meeting the needs of the people they serve.
- The information and data generated as a result of working to provide effective programs and services produces components that most grant proposals require.
- Use your success as a marketing opportunity.

Reference

Laughlin, Sara, and Ray W. Wilson. 2008. *The Quality Library: A Guide to Staff-driven Improvement, Better Efficiency, and Happier Customers*. Chicago: American Library Association.

Index

Note: Page references for figures, textboxes, worksheets, and exercises are italicized.

About the Author

Pamela H. MacKellar (www.pamelamackellar.com) is an author and library consultant who has worked in the library science field for more than thirty years. Since earning a master's degree in library science from the State University of New York at Albany, she has held positions as a newspaper librarian, library director, assistant librarian, health sciences librarian, cataloger, technology consultant, and independent consultant in libraries of all kinds including special, school, public, postsecondary, tribal, prison, and state library agency.

The author of *Writing Successful Technology Grant Proposals: A LITA Guide* (2012) and *The Accidental Librarian* (2008), Pam has also cowritten *Winning Grants: A Multimedia How-To-Do-It Manual for Librarians with Multimedia Tutorials and Grant Development Tools* (2010) and *Grants for Libraries: A How-To-Do-It Manual* (2006). She has written numerous articles and presented at many library conferences.

Pam has designed and taught online courses and workshops on grants for libraries and nonprofits, written successful proposals for government and foundation grants, planned and administered grant projects, and reviewed grant proposals for federal and state agencies. She was the recipient of the 2010 Loleta D. Fyan Award from the American Library Association for an online management course for new library directors in New Mexico.

In addition, Pam designs and creates websites for small public libraries. She lives in New Mexico with her husband and two cats, where she is also a printmaker, makes artist books, and teaches book arts classes (www.pamonpaper.com).